Becoming Her: How the Faith of Biblical Women Can Guide Your Transformation to Heal, Grow, and Walk in Your Calling

by
Dejah Smart-Moses

Foreword By Latoya Belfon- John

LABWORKS PUBLISHING

Labworks Publishing Inc.
Quebec, Canada

Becoming Her: How the Faith of Biblical Women Can Guide Your Transformation to Heal, Grow, and Walk in Your Calling

© 2025 by Dejah Smart-Moses
 All rights reserved.
ISBN: 978-1-990420-24-5

Designed & published by Labworks Publishing Inc.
Chateauguay, Quebec, Canada
www.labworkspublishing.com

Library and Archives Canada Cataloguing in Publication
A copy of this publication is available at Library and Archives Canada.

Disclaimer:
The content in this book represents the author's personal reflections and insights. Readers are encouraged to interpret and apply the information according to their own judgment and personal circumstances.

Printed in Canada
First Edition, 2025

Dedication

First and foremost, I want to thank God for all He has done and for everything He has helped me accomplish in this lifetime. This book is extremely special to me; it was birthed through the gift of the Holy Spirit. I take this moment to dedicate it to all the women who have played a meaningful and impactful role in my life.

Who I am today is largely because of the love, prayers, and wisdom of those incredible sisters, steadfast Stellas, and devoted praying mothers within our church body. I am deeply grateful and profoundly thankful for each of you.

Most importantly, I dedicate this labour of love to my mother, Myriam Pitter. You have been nothing short of a hero to me— my Esther, my Ruth, my Rebekah. You have fought for me, loved me unconditionally, covered me in prayer, and stood in the gap when I couldn't stand on my own. I am eternally grateful that God chose you to be my mother.

Lastly, I want to express my heartfelt thanks to a young lady who inspires me daily—my daughter, my mini-me, Hannah Abigail Moses. Your very presence in my life has challenged me to grow, to strive, and to become the best version of myself. You are one of my greatest blessings.

To all of you, thank you. This book is for you.

" *And* be not conformed to this world: but be ye transformed by the renewing of your mind,
  that ye may prove what is that good, and acceptable, and perfect, will of God."
— Romans 12:2 (KJV)

Welcome

Welcome, my beloved transformed women. It is my privilege and honour to walk this journey with you. I want to take this moment to create a space of truth, reflection, and encouragement, a space where we can have heartfelt conversations and engage in meaningful reflections that inspire you to become the best version of yourself.

This book is an invitation to engage deeply in the process that God is leading you through. It is a guide to help you surrender your struggles, release your trauma, and begin to live with intention, pursuing purpose and walking boldly into every dream God has planted within you.

As a wife, a mother, and above all, a woman of God, I have lived through seasons that could have broken me in every way. But the truth is this: God was always with me. What looked like breaking was actually birthing, a version of me that God saw from the very beginning.

A woman with the heart of a servant.

A woman rooted in prayer.

A woman passionate about the healing and purpose of others, and now here we are on this sacred journey.

I invite you to walk with me as we go deeper into understanding who you are becoming.

Becoming Her.

Dejah Smart Moses

Foreword

It's not often you can say that someone has journeyed with you through some of your darkest moments, and that someone isn't your spouse. I vividly remember a season of deep pain and disillusionment. I sat on crowded church benches, scanned the smiling, righteous faces, and searched YouTube for sermons and DIY healing remedies. I was desperately looking for something or for someone who would know what to say to help me navigate a moment where, despite my faith and works, God seemed painfully silent.

The disconnect between the promises I read in the Word and the reality I lived left me spiralling. That silence suffocated me. And when I finally came up for air, even the air felt like it rejected me. Once again, I searched for someone who truly understood that kind of spiritual ache. Someone transparent enough to meet me in my low place and pull me up.

That's when I staggered over to her one Sunday morning —Evangelist Dejah Smart-Moses. I was on the brink. Life felt too heavy to carry. And like Hannah, whose desperation for a miracle made her appear drunk, I was undone. I needed a word from God. And through her, I received it. I clung to those words until my promise came into view.

Evangelist Dejah Smart-Moses has stood in the gap for so many, interceding with boldness, weeping with those who weep, and warring in the Spirit until breakthrough comes. Her life is an offering of grace, love, and service—

a living testament to what it means to honour God in all things. Like me, many women of faith live with unanswered questions, silent seasons, and unmet expectations. We crave connection, guidance, and real testimony from someone who's been through the fire.

That's why, when Ev. Dejah shared her vision to reach women through an annual women's conference (Transformation Conference), I knew this was only the beginning of something deeply needed. But most of all, I knew this was her answering her divine calling.

From the vision of the Transformation Conference, *"Becoming Her"*, the book was born. *"Becoming Her"* became a beacon of hope, a weapon of warfare, and a mirror, one that showed me both who I was and who I was becoming. It revealed the areas of my life that needed healing and growth, while extending grace to the woman I was still learning to love and accept. It called me gently but firmly into purpose, reminding me that even in my imperfect journey, I am still a child of God, and He's not done with me yet.

Ev. Dejah has masterfully combined timeless scripture with raw personal insight. These biblical women's stories, reframed with present-day revelation, speak directly to modern women who desire to be equipped with the truth of God's Word. *"Becoming Her"* reminds us that although no woman is perfect, we are being perfected daily, by grace, for His glory.

This book testifies to God's power to take the broken, the overlooked, the complicated, the unlikely, and transform them into kingdom warriors. It speaks to the woman who feels unworthy, unseen, or stuck in a version of herself that doesn't align with the divine blueprint God has written.

Through Ev. Dejah's voice, we hear God's call again:

You are chosen.

You are becoming.

So, dear sister, take courage. Lay down the weight. Like Mary Magdalene, receive your deliverance. Like Hannah, cry out in fervent prayer. Like Deborah, rise in wisdom and prepare for battle. If this book declares anything, it's that God can use you, anywhere, anytime, at any stage, if you're willing to become the vessel who says YES.

Say yes... to Becoming Her.

Latoya Belfon

Best-selling author, Publishing expert, & IP Strategist | Creator of the Resource-Driven Strategy Methodology™

Table of CONTENTS

INTRODUCTION   1

TRANSFORMED TO PROMINENCE   6

TRANSFORMED FROM BARRENNESS   25

ON TIME TRANSFORMATION   42

TRANSFORMED TO PRESERVE DESTINY   58

TRANSFORMED TO COVENANT   71

TRANSFORMED TO SUBMISSION   84

TRANSFORMED BY FAITH   98

TRANSFORMED THROUGH REJECTION   114

TRANSFORMED THROUGH MENTORSHIP   129

A TRANSFORMED LEADER   143

YOU ARE HER   168

Introduction

Sometime in February 2023, during a time of prayer in my husband's prayer room, I had an encounter with God. It was something I had never experienced before, an intense awareness of God's presence in the room and Him speaking to me profoundly. I was like a babe, not knowing what to do. Overwhelmed, I wanted to call someone —my husband, my mother, anyone to pray and help me carry the weight of what I was feeling.

As I lay there with my eyes closed, I saw a vision. In that vision, I saw women gathered and worshipping. It was not in a church setting, but in a large space that felt like a hotel. It was so profound I could not deny it, even if I wanted to. At that moment, I decided to rest in that sacred space and receive the Lord. It was not just a moment of receiving; it was a moment of surrender, surrendering to God and what He wanted. I surrendered my will, my fears, and my insecurities, and I decided to be and do whatever He said. It felt like all I knew was to be in Christ, and now it was time to walk in it. I was reaffirmed and recommissioned by God. I was becoming her.

As I continued to worship God, I became more broken and humbled, rocking myself back and forth. I heard the word "Transformation" and kept seeing the large gathering of women. It was a terrifying and humbling feeling.

An overwhelming surge of emotions flowed through me. The fear of how and when tried to creep into my thoughts, but I chose silence, silence so as not to speak against what God was doing. Silence because I understood that this was a God moment, a divine moment, and I was apprehensive to say anything that might violate what God was doing in me. I knew it was God, and the only response was to say, Yes! Yes, Lord! Yes to purpose! Yes, to tuning in to what He was saying and what the mandate was. Yes, to adjusting myself and prioritizing what God required of me.

We cannot allow ourselves to rush the process or ad-lib for God, perverting or filtering what God's directives are. The only decision to make was to move forward with grace and humility.

Sweet embrace, that moment of embracing the vision and responding to the mandate of doing a women's conference had lifted the weight of His presence that I felt in that room. I'm going to be honest: I held on to that moment and that word for such a long time, only sharing it with one person. I wanted to ensure that when I spoke, it would be in the moment and time that God wanted me to. I endeavoured to embrace and understand what the vision was.

The scriptures clearly say, "Where there is no vision, the people perish: but he that keepeth the law, happy is he." (Proverbs 29:18, KJV) Therefore, it was my responsibility not to speak without having a complete understanding.
I needed clarity, not just in hearing, but in expressing and verbalizing what God showed me and what I heard.

Transformation, according to the Oxford English Dictionary, is a thorough, dramatic change in appearance, character, or form.

You see, as a transformed woman, you need to know when to speak and when to be silent. We cannot rush to the finish line. Receiving and hearing the vision is just part of the mandate; communicating it is another layer. I spent the next few weeks and months carrying the word in my spirit, and I waited. I allowed God to mature the word and solidify the vision in my heart.

Can you imagine if I had run around with the vision He gave me and spoke of it untimely—in ears, spaces, and times that were not able to receive or embrace it? It is His vision, not mine. I am just the messenger—the one whom God graced and delegated to carry it out. God needs to know He can trust us, not just to hear, but to walk in obedience to every single directive. He needs to know we will follow instructions, not just receive them.

Hearing is important, but your response is just as vital to the process of God using you to transform lives. The scriptures state in Romans 10:17, "So then faith cometh by hearing, and hearing by the word of God."
It is when you hear a direct word from God that your faith can be lifted. It is when the unction of God can be solidified in your spirit and manifest in your life.
Though fear may try to creep in, you can stand on His word and be reassured.

I left my fetal position in that room with my faith lifted and fortified, knowing that no one could convince me otherwise. All I needed to do was respond with obedience. No one was going to deter me. No one was going to say no. No one was going to discourage me from what I heard and saw.

I chose to move forward in God and prayed that He would tell me when and who. That day, I walked out a transformed woman with a testimony to share.   3

The next few decisions were just as important as the hearing. What I did was walk in silence. Out of my need to be obedient, I had to be silent. I spoke only to one other person. That conversation was brief but safe. During that time, God strategically sent several individuals who would confirm His vision. After nine months of carrying this vision, I was confronted, and I heard it was time.

I began to share it with one sister-friend and family member, who instantly embraced the vision. After that moment, everyone I spoke to was someone I felt in my heart was the right person to share it with. Every single individual grabbed hold of that vision.

No one spoke a word of doubt or questioned its validity. It was as if they had heard the vision too and wanted to see it come to pass.

I believe that when someone is transformed, they are now functioning at their highest potential or ability. It causes us to see things through a particular lens based on who we are and how we show up in a specific space.

I truly believe that we are in a season of *TRANSFORMATION*. This is not by choice but by divine order. God wants to transform us by the renewing of our minds, but also through our identity. He not only wants us to be transformed, but to be agents of transformation.

Who you are and who you identify as, as an individual, matters because that is how you show up in life. That is how you show up as a believer, a mother, a friend, a wife, a sister, and a colleague. Your identity speaks of who you are, your individuality, and your uniqueness. It speaks of your values. Through your identity and unique qualities, God will use you to effect change in and around you.

When you begin to see your identity through God's eyes, transformation becomes inevitable.

4

The way you show up in every role is shaped by how you understand who He says you are, not just who you've been, but who you're becoming. This journey isn't about chasing perfection or titles; it's about stepping into the version of yourself that is needed for such a time as this. It's about surrendering to His design so you can carry out divine assignments with clarity, courage, and purpose. That is the heartbeat of Becoming Her.

Becoming Her is not a single moment; it is a transformational process. It is becoming the woman God envisioned before the world ever saw you. She is not who the world told her to be; she is who God called her to become. She is formed for purpose, set apart for divine assignment, and empowered to disrupt generational cycles, build Kingdom legacy, and ignite transformation everywhere she walks.

Throughout this book, we will explore the lives of women who embraced transformation by understanding their identity in God and, as a result, sparked profound change around them. Like most of the women we will examine throughout this book, I want you to begin to reflect on who you are and how God can use your weaknesses, mistakes, and tragedies, but most of all, your character, to bring about transformation in your life.

It is time for us to become her: the Her He desires you to be.

Mary Magdalene

Transformed to Prominence

*Mary was a woman who was undervalued, but with one
encounter with Jesus, her life was transformed and
memorialized by Christ.*

Set Free!

Mary is one of the most profoundly transformed
women in the Bible. Her transformation is undeniable and
is revealed throughout her story. When we are first
introduced to her, she is described as a woman possessed
by seven demons—an affliction from which Jesus delivered
her, as recorded in Luke chapter 8.

To truly understand the depth of Mary's transformation,
we must consider the daily torment she endured. As a
woman possessed by multiple demons, she likely endured
extreme emotional turmoil, depression, rejection,
oppression, and deep uncertainty. We can only imagine
how often she questioned her value and worth, asking
herself, "When will this end? Will I ever live a normal life?"

Although my story differs from Mary's, I cannot count
the number of times I asked God, "When will it be my
turn? When will I get to enjoy life without constant
difficulty?"

6

But just as with Mary, one encounter with Jesus changed everything. Her life was never the same. She was not only delivered from demonic possession but was transformed into a woman who began to see herself through the eyes of Christ. She became free!

Mary no longer carried the burden of depression, oppression, or rejection. She was no longer the woman shunned by society, labelled a prostitute, and ostracized by the men of her community. Her transformation is evident in the scripture when she walked with him, served alongside and bore witness to His ministry. Mary was not an outsider; she was a part of the inner circle of Christ.

"After this, Jesus traveled about from one town and village to another, proclaiming the good news of the kingdom of God. The Twelve were with him, 2 and also some women who had been cured of evil spirits and diseases: Mary (called Magdalene) from whom seven demons had come out."

LUKE 8 VS 1-2

But Jesus does not see us as the world sees us. He sees us as the Father sees us. He sees our gifts, our potential, and the good within us. We all have a past and bear the labels society places upon us.

Yet, we must bring ourselves before the Father, seek Jesus, and receive His transforming power. We must rise above our past and step into our God-given destiny. An encounter with Christ can transform your life, just as it did for Mary.

I remember that early in my ministry, many saw me as unapproachable and hardened. But over the years, as I grew closer to God—through deeper intimacy with Him and life's many challenges, I was transformed.
I became more tender-hearted and approachable, while still maintaining the anointing and my moral integrity. God is fully able to take the most painful, difficult parts of our lives and transform us into beautiful, faithful servants.

Dedicated Supporter

Mary met Jesus at a very low point in her life—it may be safe to say that she was at rock bottom, possessed by seven demons. Her transformation was profound and evident after that one meeting. It was clear that Mary embraced her transformation and decided to live a changed life. She did not retreat to her old ways or adopt a self-centred mentality of "I am free to just do me." Instead, she took her freedom and became a supporter of Jesus' ministry.

Mary, among other women, followed and journeyed with Christ as He ministered on earth, not only in proximity, but also with her substance.
When we stop to think about that one encounter—being possessed by seven demons, and then finally being free— imagine what that must have felt like. After years of torment, someone finally touches your life in a way no one ever has. Someone ministers to you, speaks to you, delivers you, and frees you from your torment.

Could it be that the "seven" demons represent more than just a number? That the number seven, biblically meaning complete or whole, signified Mary being completely delivered—mind, body, and soul—from the tortures and trauma of her past?

Today, I propose to you that God wants you to be free in the same way. Just as Mary was set free from everything that tormented her, He wants to set you free from whatever limits you from becoming who you are called to be. The version of you that the enemy desperately wants to stop is the version God is shaping and forming. I pause and present to you today: you, too, can be free. God desires your complete freedom. Mary responded to her deliverance with gratitude, demonstrated through her dedication to serve alongside Christ. She went where He went, sat where He sat, ate what He ate, saw the people He saw. She served not only Jesus but His disciples as well, and she didn't do it alone. She served in community with other women.

It is important to note that Mary didn't just show up in service, she showed out. She was constantly in proximity to Christ, but she also gave of herself financially. She supported Jesus' ministry with her own resources. Scripture names her first among the women, signifying her leadership and prominence in how she served Christ. Her gratitude, her discipline, her generosity, and her physical presence all pointed to her deep devotion. Mary was more than just a woman who walked beside Jesus; she was a true disciple.

In the context of the time, it was highly uncommon for a woman to be acknowledged for her financial contributions. But Mary did it because she believed. She knew what one encounter with Jesus could do. Others may not have recognized the value of her support, but Jesus did. It was significant in His eyes, so much so that He chose her to be the first to witness and testify of His resurrection.

Her dedication endured. She remained by His side during His ministry, His trial, His crucifixion, His burial—and even after all others had left, she was still there. A supporter. A servant. A disciple.

"Joanna the wife of Chuza, the manager of Herod's household; Susanna; and many others. These women were helping to support them out of their own means.."

LUKE 8 VS 3

Like Mary, who gave her best to Christ, we too are called to serve Him with our best. We must make the intentional choice to offer Christ our highest worship, our most faithful service, and the best version of ourselves. It is essential that we show up in society, in our churches, and in our families, with excellence and purpose.

Mary Magdalene poured out her life in unwavering devotion to Jesus, refusing to let the labels of her past or the whispers of others define her. Her service was not driven by obligation; it was her most valuable offering. It was her sacrifice. A pure expression of gratitude to the One who had delivered her completely.

When we serve with such purpose and intention, it becomes a powerful demonstration of our love and passion for Christ. That kind of wholehearted devotion draws others in. It inspires them to love Him and desire to serve Him as well. We are meant to be living examples of what it looks like to serve Christ passionately and faithfully. 10

Our love for Christ and the way we serve Him should never be dependent on how others choose to serve. There should be no limits to our devotion. We are called to serve in the best way we can—serving with integrity, with passion, and with a love that flows from a personal relationship with our Saviour, the One we love.

When we are truly transformed, we are moved to live differently. Transformation is not just inward; it must be visible in how we act and serve. Without question, Mary's outward acts of love and service reflected an inward transformation. Something within her heart had been changed so radically that it could not help but show on the outside.

Over the years, as I evolved from a young worshipper to a more intentional servant, I, too, can see the transformation in my life—the growth, and the impact it has on others.

" I, too, became a servant in His Kingdom.

In becoming the woman that I am today, it was through years of acts of service—serving the body of Christ in more ways than one. It wasn't just about showing up to a church service, lifting my hands, singing songs, or worshipping God in word. It was about showing up for people—cleaning the floors, serving meals, preparing meals, shaking hands, greeting strangers, and praying at the altar. I chose the work that comes with ministry. I chose service.

I chose it because I love God. My heart has always been grateful to Him. And just like Mary, whose life was transformed after one powerful encounter with Jesus, my heart was also transformed into the heart of a servant. I, too, became a servant in His Kingdom.

Walking In Purpose!

As a transformed woman, Mary Magdalene was the first person to show up at Jesus's tomb. Again, we see her faithfulness as a servant by showing up to complete burial rituals amid her grieving and great loss. When you show up where you need to be, you are positioning yourself for unexpected blessings. It was at this moment that she was chosen to be the first to see Jesus. She did not wait for anyone to give her directives. She did not wait on the other apostles; she took the initiative and moved forward based on her love for Christ and the new direction her life was going.

We need to move when God says move. We need to get our directives from God and serve the Kingdom as God is directing us.

> "Jesus said, 'Do not hold on to me, for I have not yet ascended to the Father. Go instead to my brothers and tell them, 'I am ascending to my Father and your Father, to my God and your God."

JOHN 20 VS 17

Mary was the first to share the message of His resurrection. She rose early and went to the tomb, where she learned that He was risen and no longer in the grave.

The message of His resurrection was first preached by Mary to the apostles. Often, we hear that women should not do this or do that in churches—that women should not lead or teach—but here we see that Jesus commissioned her to go to the apostles and let them know that He is alive, that He is risen!

According to John 20:17, by this act, it is safe to say she preached and shared the first message of Jesus's resurrection. I cannot say it more clearly: Mary's transformation prompted her to act on her purpose, not her past. She was not intimidated by her role as a woman or by the accusations she had faced in the past. She was inclined to be and do what God transformed her to be.

We do not know why Christ chose Mary. But if I were to imagine—could it be because she showed up when everyone else did not in that moment? Could it be that she was consistently present at His death, burial, and resurrection? Could it be that she spared no expenses and served Him with all of who she was and with her means? Or could it be that she sought Him in a place of death, agony, and darkness?

God will show up and reveal Himself to us when we seek after Him in our moments of agony, despair, desolation, and in our dark moments.

Your Identity Matters

One of the many significant things about Mary's life is that, though Jesus chose twelve apostles, Mary can be seen as one of the disciples of Jesus, as He had many. Jesus had many followers and disciples, and Mary Magdalene was one of the most notable, as her name is often mentioned in the scriptures.

It is understood that there is importance to names in the scriptures. How often a name is mentioned in the Bible indicates the standing or significance of the person. Mary's name was mentioned more often than that of most of the other disciples and apostles, which speaks to her value and importance in Jesus' ministry on earth. She was one of the disciples who was present at His death, burial, and resurrection, in addition to supporting His ministry financially. Her prominence in Jesus's ministry was undeniable.

When you are transformed, it does not matter who knows you or who calls your name—it is more important who names you. That is what counts. We are to rise early and go in the name of Jesus, knowing that He will establish us and cause us to evolve. It is more important that Jesus knows your name, and it is your acts of dedicated, sacrificial service poured out onto Christ that will establish you.

Mary was once known as a prostitute, possessed by demons; she is now known as a woman who served and dedicated her life to support Jesus's ministry while here on earth.

"Do not allow others to use your past against you. Know who you are in Christ. It is in Christ that you find your identity, not in the opinion of others."

Life may often treat us unfairly. You may be made to feel less significant than you are, and that you have little or no value or worth. Mary was denigrated by the men in her community; nonetheless, it is important to know that from God's perspective, you are worthy, by the blood of Jesus!

When Jesus transformed her life, Mary Magdalene responded with unwavering devotion. She followed Him closely, not just in proximity, but with purpose—serving with her resources, her presence, and her whole heart. Her life became a public declaration of love for the One who had changed everything. She didn't allow whispers or judgment to stop her. Instead, she poured out her loyalty and commitment, offering her best to the Saviour who had seen her, healed her, and called her.

Once you allow Christ to come into your life, and He has freed you from the past, it is for you to appropriate that freedom and not allow the enemy of your soul to use your past to hold you captive. Do not allow others to use your past against you. Know who you are in Christ. It is in Christ that you find your identity, not in the opinions of others. He has saved you for a purpose, and He has given you a mandate in this life. It is your obligation and responsibility to walk out your transformation.

Even in society, people will look down on you, discredit you, and undermine your value and worth. But God wants to remind you: what He says is more important than what the people of the world say. He has given you your identity, and He sees you as important and valuable.

'Therefore if any man be in Christ, he is a new creature: old things are passed away; behold, all things are become new."

2 CORINTHIANS 5:17

He is your Creator. He is the Author and Finisher of your soul! Mary did not wait for anyone to give her permission to begin her service. Once she was transformed, she ran boldly and served Christ with her proximity, with her finances, and in every capacity she could.

She was present and bore witness to His death, His burial, and His resurrection as she walked the journey with Him. We have a duty to serve God. Just like Mary, we must go! We are transformed to serve. Therefore, go and serve in whatever capacity you are called to.

Mary did not wait until Jesus ascended into heaven; she stepped into her divine purpose the moment she became aware, through the transforming power of Jesus.

You cannot wait for recognition to walk in purpose. There were moments in my journey when I took on roles and responsibilities simply out of a heart of obedience and servanthood. Many times while serving, I felt overlooked and dismissed. But deep within, my spirit understood the value of servanthood. And so, I chose to serve and dedicate myself fully to the ministry and God.

What can we learn from Mary? We learn that she was a woman of deep devotion. Her transformation didn't end with healing—it overflowed into a life of service, sacrifice, and presence. Mary ministered not just with her words, but with her actions, her substance, and her unwavering love for Christ. How many times has God healed us, answered our prayers, or delivered us—only for us to forget the power of what He's done? Mary didn't forget. She responded with her life. Now, it's your turn to reflect.

Becoming Her Check-In

Reflect:

What areas of my life mirror Mary's need for transformation?

What's one part of my past that I need to stop disqualifying myself for?

Where can I show up boldly—like Mary did—without waiting for permission?

Respond:

Write a short prayer or declaration of your desire to move forward, not from your past, but toward your purpose.

Time of Meditation

Allow the power of the Word of God to work on your heart and transform your life by moving you from your past into your future, your destiny. Mary was significantly misunderstood and misjudged, yet she availed herself to be transformed. All you need is an encounter with Jesus Christ. Mary had one encounter, and her life was never the same. There is a purpose that lies beneath the surface of your past and the unveiling of your destiny. It is time to break free and be transformed.

Scriptures

---❖---

2 Corinthians 5:17

Therefore if any man be in Christ, he is a new creature: old things are passed away; behold, all things are become new.

Romans 8:1

There is therefore now no condemnation to them which are in Christ Jesus, who walk not after the flesh, but after the Spirit.

Luke 11: 4

And forgive us our sins; for we also forgive every one that is indebted to us. And lead us not into temptation; but deliver us from evil.

1 John 1:9

If we confess our sins, he is faithful and just to forgive us our sins, and to cleanse us from all unrighteousness.

Hebrew 12:2

Looking unto Jesus the author and finisher of our faith; who for the joy that was set before him endured the cross, despising the shame, and is set down at the right hand of the throne of God.

Action Steps to
Transformation

What are some things you carry from your past that leave room for condemnation in your life? You must be intentional about breaking free from your past and recognize that it is through the blood of Jesus Christ and the power of His Word that true freedom is found.

_____
_____
_____
_____
_____
_____
_____
_____
_____
_____
_____
_____

Action Steps to
Transformation

There are some practical steps you can take to free yourself from past mistakes. What are they? I cannot emphasize enough the importance of identifying them by name and then allowing the Spirit of God to lead you through the process of laying them down.

_____
_____
_____
_____
_____
_____
_____
_____
_____
_____
_____
_____
_____

Action Steps to
Transformation

What are some ways you can serve in the body of Christ—areas where you know you are gifted and that can create opportunities for you to serve? Like Mary, you need to go by using your gift. Too often, we overlook our God-given talents and ignore the fact that they are a great starting point for serving in the body of Christ.

I encourage you to take time to list a few things you are good at and passionate about presenting to God. Then, seek Him earnestly and ask Him to show you how to use your gifts to serve.

_____

_____

_____

_____

_____

_____

_____

_____

_____

A
PRAYER
For You!

Lord, I ask You to forgive me for judging myself and not looking to You as the Author and Finisher of my faith. I thank You for sending Jesus, who made the ultimate sacrifice to forgive me of my sin and my past transgressions. Help me to embrace my new freedom and to dedicate my life to living for You in abundance.

Guide me into fulfilling my destiny as a transformed woman, knowing that old things have passed away and all things are made new. I commit my destiny and every plan You have for my life into Your hands. It is my desire to live a life of service to You each and every day. Guide me in identifying areas where I can serve You intentionally and effectively— where I will impact the lives of those around me. Help me to make room for You in my life and to serve You faithfully, as Mary did. I let go of everything in my past—anything that would hold me back from moving forward and embracing the transformation You are executing in my life. Father, I yield my will to You as I endeavour to walk in obedience to Your divine will.
Amen.

surrender

Key Takeaways

Transformation

✓ Seek clarity

✓ Take action

✓ Trust God

Becoming Her: Devoted

What began as a cry to silence her torment became a life of unwavering devotion—marked by bold proximity, costly sacrifice, and love that spoke louder than her past.

notes

Hannah

Transformed from Barrenness to Birthing a Prophet.

~~~~~~~~~~

Hannah went years without bearing children and wept bitterly as she was mocked and looked down on. Yet through steadfast intercession, she received her blessing in an extraordinary way —by giving birth to a prophet.

The Desire

To understand Hannah and her transformation, we must understand her story. Hannah was barren for many years, and although she was dearly loved by her husband, he did not fully grasp the depth of her agony. It was easy for him to dismiss the pain of childlessness because his other wife had borne children for him, and that same wife made Hannah's life nothing short of a living hell. The love he had for Hannah rivalled his lack of understanding, but despite his affection and the opposition she faced, Hannah's desire for children never left her. In fact, it seemed to grow stronger every day.

Hannah lived in a time when having children was considered a woman's main responsibility, and not being able to fulfil that role was seen as shameful. Just like Hannah, many women today face infertility and reproductive challenges that leave them emotionally crippled and spiritually depleted.

The burden of unmet expectations, internalized feelings of failure, and society's unrelenting ridicule is heavy for any woman to bear. Yet Hannah's longing to carry her child only deepened, often bringing her to tears.

There are things we are each believing God for. For some, it's a child. For others, it may be a spouse, healing, or deliverance. Whatever your longing is, hold on to it. Do not allow anyone to dismiss your desire or bully you out of it. Like Hannah, keep the faith, and be steadfast in your pursuit.

> "Confess your faults one to another, and pray one for another, that ye may be healed. The effectual fervent prayer of a righteous man availeth much."
>
> JAMES 5 VS 16

Her Consistency

If there were one word to describe Hannah, it would be fervent. Hannah was passionate and enthusiastic about her desire. She was not passive, inconsistent, or inactive regarding what she wanted, despite the opposition she faced. The Bible says in James 5:16, "Confess your faults one to another, and pray one for another, that ye may be healed. The effectual fervent prayer of a righteous man availeth much."

Hannah experienced transformation through her persistence in prayer and her consistency in her role as a wife. When we examine Hannah's story, we see a woman living in a time when childbearing was a defining and pivotal role of a wife.

26

There was immense pressure from society, extended family, and often from the husband himself to produce children. In Hannah's case, she had none.

As a result, Hannah battled internally, facing thoughts of never having a child of her own and feelings of self-blame. What did I do wrong? I imagine Hannah often having to speak to herself to stay encouraged and not fall into deep depression. It seemed she had no one who truly understood what she was experiencing. Her husband, Elkanah, tried to comfort her, but his efforts fell short. Though compassionate and loving, he lacked a full understanding of the deep, ingrained desire Hannah had to bear children.

To make matters worse, Hannah had a co-wife, Peninnah, who was neither compassionate nor kind. At every opportunity, Peninnah attacked Hannah's infertility, provoking her bitterly and adding to her sorrow. Hannah's pain was persistent, but so was her prayer.

> "And as he did so year by year, when she went up to the house of the Lord, so she provoked her; therefore she wept, and did not eat."
>
> I SAMUEL I VS7

Though Hannah was sorrowful, she did not allow her sorrow to deter her from moving forward. As a wife, she accompanied her husband to the temple, as they did yearly. As transformed women, we cannot allow our current circumstances to stop us from being who we are and doing what we ought in the moments we are called upon. Like Hannah, we must persevere and press forward.

27

Hannah took her place as his wife and journeyed with him each year. Despite Peninnah's provocation and Elkanah's lack of understanding of her desire, she still went to the temple—year after year. Often, when we face difficult and trying times in life, we want to walk away and give up—on our dreams, our marriages, our children, our careers, and even our purpose.

We cannot allow sorrow or the tragedies of life to stop us from pursuing God and the desires of our hearts. There are things in you that only you and God know about, and it is up to you to be fervent in your pursuit to see those things come to manifestation. Only Hannah knew the depth of her desire; therefore, only she could pursue it with such fervency.

Her Drunken Prayer

"And she was in bitterness of soul,
and prayed unto the Lord, and wept sore."

I SAMUEL I VS 10

Hannah persevered and went to Shiloh. Rather than hide in some corner, she went to the temple and prayed. She prayed fervently—so fervently that she was accused of being drunk by the priest. Her lips moved, but no sound came out. For her presence in the house of God to resemble that of a drunk person, we can only imagine how deep into prayer she must have been, lost in intercession, oblivious to those around her.

28

She didn't care who was watching. Her body likely swayed and staggered in uncoordinated movements, enough for the priest to assume she was intoxicated.

There are some things in life we must contend for—not in the natural, but in the spiritual. Hannah used the spiritual tool of prayer to access the gift of God. She prayed passionately, intensely, and with a broken heart. Her weeping moved God to speak through the priest, who prophesied that she would have a son.

As a woman living a transformed life, you must understand that it is not only your responsibility to show up for and with your husband, but also to show up for God, for yourself! When you show up in the presence of God, He will show up for you in a mighty way.

As transformed women, we must use biblical principles to pursue the desires of our hearts. We cannot allow the pressures of life to compel us to seek help outside the Kingdom of God. While everyone else was eating, Hannah was praying. While they were drinking, Hannah was praying. While they were socializing, Hannah was praying. The spiritual tools of prayer, fasting, and presenting herself before God in the temple were her weapons of choice.

Because Hannah was persistent in prayer, God remembered her. He remembered that He had shut her womb, and He decided it was time—time to transition Hannah into her season of blessing. It was time to end her torment and agony. Hannah did not take for granted that her husband was a godly man who offered sacrifices each year. Nor did she assume that God would simply "do it" for her. She forged forward with fervent, consistent prayer. And because of that, God showed up. He will show up for you, too. He will remember you. He will grant you the desires of your heart. The very thing they laughed at you about—the thing you thought you would never receive, the reason you feared God had forgotten you.

He is about to remember, and He is about to answer.

Despite everything Hannah endured, she never gave up. She pursued her purpose through consistent, fervent prayer. I encourage you today: don't give up. Pursue your purpose. Pursue God. Pray with passion and persistence.

Answered Prayer

"In the midst of her antagonist, Hannah now carried the visible manifestation of her transformation."

Can you imagine what it feels like to finally receive the very thing you've been praying and waiting for for years? Hannah does! She received the desire of her heart: a son, Samuel.

Hannah took the spoken word of prophecy from the priest and ran with it. Her consistency and fervency in prayer brought her into alignment with heaven, where God released a word just for her. Sometimes, all we need is one word from God. A word that can transform our sorrow into joy, our barrenness into fruitfulness, and our waiting into fulfilment.

Hannah, once barren, depressed, bitter, and sorrowful, is now pregnant with the very thing she wept for. In the face of her antagonist, she carried the visible manifestation of her transformation. She returned home with her husband, fulfilled her role as a wife, and conceived.

That child would become the prophet who anointed the first king of Israel—King David—through whose lineage came our Lord and Saviour, Jesus Christ.

God will use your tragedy and transform it for purpose. The very agony Hannah experienced became the catalyst for the elevation of her prayer life and her faith.

Let's take a moment to focus on Hannah's response to both her antagonist and her deep yearning for a child.

Hannah's response was not retaliation.

It was not gossip.

It was not complaining.

Hannah's response was prayer.

She didn't bring her needs to the priest. She didn't even bring it to her husband. Hannah had a personal relationship with God, and she poured her desire directly into the hands of the One who could do something about it. She laid out her pain, her feelings of failure, and her agony in a desperate plea before God, asking Him to remember her.

She didn't respond to Peninnah's immature mockery year after year. She chose to take her emotions, not to people, but to the throne of grace. Even when she was in the temple, she didn't seek out the priest. It was the priest who found her already in deep intercession.

As transformed women, we must adopt this same posture. When trials press in and desires feel delayed, our first response must be to God.

Not people.

Not the world.

Not panic.

We bring our hearts, our hopes, and our hurts to the Father. Yes, there are anointed people around us, and yes, God can use them. But before we seek the counsel of others, let us seek the counsel of God. Ask Him to guide your step, even in who you share your burdens with.

God should always be our first choice.

A Womb Shut

The Bible said God had shut her womb. But even that was intentional. God used the closed door to draw Hannah into a deeper level of intercession. It was in that place of brokenness and surrender that her prayers were no longer ordinary; they became transformational.

Her pain pushed her into the presence of God, and in that presence, she received peace. Before the promise was fulfilled, peace entered her spirit. That word from God became her confirmation.

There are times in our lives when God delays the blessing because it is not an ordinary blessing. It is one that will bring about a generational impact. One that will require preparation and a stretching of our faith.

Hannah's answer to her prayers brought forth the prophet Samuel. And Samuel didn't just change Hannah's life—he changed the course of Israel's history. He was the one who anointed King David, and through David's lineage came the Messiah.

God used Hannah's pain to birth a prophet.

And through that prophet came a king.

And through that king came the Saviour of the world.

What might God be forming through your tears?

"Like Hannah, I prayed for several years for a child. Like Hannah, I fasted and prayed."

Hannah walked through her transformation and into her destiny, directly linking her to Jesus Christ. That said, her destiny is memorialized through Jesus Christ even today as we speak.

Hannah's transformation happened when she received the word from the priest, and her countenance changed from desperately unhappy to radiant.

If there is a story in the Bible that I identify with, it would be the story of Hannah. That is why my daughter was named Hannah. Like Hannah, I prayed for several years for a child. Like Hannah, I fasted and prayed. Like Hannah, I felt ridicule—literally. Like Hannah, I received a word. And like Hannah, I knew my husband, and God blessed us with a child and now children.

This story was deeply inspiring to me, as I too experienced a season of having a shut womb. Hannah's story shifted my spiritual perspective, teaching me how to pray fervently, even when there was no visible evidence that my prayers were being answered. Hannah means 'grace,' and despite the profound impact this biblical story had on my life, I also wanted my daughter, Hannah, to carry that legacy. I wanted her to walk proudly, knowing that it was only by God's grace and mercy that she was brought into this world.

She is purposed, chosen, and by no means insignificant.

Becoming Her Check- In

Reflect:

Have you allowed your pain to bring you into the presence of God, like Hannah did?

Are you willing to pray fervently—not casually, but passionately and persistently—until transformation comes?

Who can you invite to join you in agreement to strengthen your prayer life and faith journey?

Respond:

Write down one area of your life where you feel barren, and how you can begin to pray over it with faith today.

Time of Meditation

It is time to meditate. In this section, I invite you to reflect on the scripture and how you are a transformed woman. Do not allow the things around you to distract you from moving forward in life and carrying out your destiny. Transformation may take time, but as women of God, we must be patient through the process. Hannah's strategy was prayer—she chose to pray and not focus on her enemy.

Scriptures

❖

James 5:16
Confess your faults one to another, and pray one for another, that ye may be healed. The effectual fervent prayer of a righteous man availeth much.

Philippians 4:6
Be careful for nothing; but in every thing by prayer and supplication with thanksgiving let your requests be made known unto God.

Psalms 143:1
Hear my prayer, O Lord, give ear to my supplications: in thy faithfulness answer me, and in thy righteousness.

Action Steps to
Transformation

In life, as we go through our different journeys, there are things we will desire, and we may not receive them immediately. Like Hannah, we must choose a God-given path to seek the answers we long for. What are some things you desire that you have not yet fervently prayed for? The first step is to identify them by creating a clear and precise list.

_____

_____

_____

_____

_____

_____

_____

_____

_____

_____

_____

_____

_____

Action Steps to
Transformation

It is now strategy time! Now that you have your list, it is time to create a plan for how, when, and where you will begin to pray for the things you are desiring. There are various ways to approach this, but you need to decide on the time, place, and scriptures you will use when presenting your desires to the Lord. It is important that we do not ignore the waiting period, as transformation takes time.

_____

_____

_____

_____

_____

_____

_____

_____

_____

_____

Action Steps to
Transformation

In my personal life, one of the prayer strategies I have used is having someone come into agreement with me. I challenge you to identify two or three people you could ask to come into agreement with you, to pray for the things you are waiting for and the very desires of your heart.

_____

_____

_____

_____

_____

_____

_____

_____

_____

_____

_____

_____

_____

A
PRAYER
For You!

Lord Jesus, as my sister makes her request known unto You today, it is Your Word that we lean on, as it states that You will give us the desires of our hearts. I come into agreement that You will hear her heart's cry and the fervency of her supplication unto You today.

I pray that she will not allow her negative experiences, the thoughts of others, or the words of her adversary to take hold of who she is or deter her from her destiny. Rather, she will seek after You in prayer, make her supplication known, and allow You to transform her life and bring her into her purpose. She will commit herself and dedicate her time to fervent prayer—not just prayer, but passionate, consistent intercession. My prayer is that she will find strength in her time of waiting. And as she waits upon You, O Lord, may she experience full transformation, even before the answer comes.

I pray that her countenance will radiate the change taking place in her life. She will walk in every promise and move forward as You have called her to be.

In Jesus' mighty name, Amen.

Intercession

Key Takeaways

Transformation

✓ Be Fervent in Prayer

✓ Practice Godly Principles

✓ Trust God for the Answer

Becoming Her: Fervent

What began as a cry from the depths of despair became a declaration of faith—her fervent prayers unlocking a destiny that echoed through generations.

notes

Esther

Transformed for Such a Time as This!
Change Happens When you Show Up.

⟡

Esther was positioned uniquely, chosen to intercede for her people at a pivotal moment in history. As she prepared to do the unthinkable—enter the king's court without being summoned— she demonstrated courage, purpose, and unwavering faith.

Unprecedented Favour

Esther was a young Jewish woman living in Persia, known by two names—Hadassah in Hebrew, and Esther in Persian. This dual identity is significant, as it reflects the balance she had to walk between two worlds: her hidden heritage and her public role. What stands out about Esther is what I like to call unprecedented favour. She carried favour even in the midst of personal tragedy. After the loss of her parents, Esther was lovingly taken in and raised by her cousin Mordecai, who became a father figure to her in a foreign land. She found favour again when she was selected as one of the young maidens brought to the palace as a potential queen of Persia.

Upon entering the palace, Esther's favour continued to shine. She quickly gained the approval of Hegai, the official in charge of the women, and was granted special treatment, given seven attendants and the best accommodations.

42

During her year of preparation, she stood out, earning the admiration of all who encountered her. Esther didn't force or manufacture this favour; she walked into it. I believe this favour was divinely ordained. God was positioning her for a set of unprecedented circumstances that would require an extraordinary measure of grace and favour to navigate.

> "And the king loved Esther above all the women, and she obtained grace and favour in his sight more than all the virgins; so that he set the royal crown upon her head, and made her queen instead of Vashti."

ESTHER 2 VS 17

The king and those who encountered Esther did not just favour her because of her beauty, but because of her character - her respectful and compliant nature. She was humble and obedient to her cousin's direction not to reveal her identity as a Jew, as he had instructed. She was brave —"If I perish, I perish." Esther was willing to do whatever it took to help her nation, regardless of the cost—even her own life.

Having favour is no small thing in a kingdom where you did not originate. You see, Esther was a Jew in a foreign land that was opposed to the Jewish nation. Therefore, having favour was extremely beneficial for Esther, as her environment was about to become a hostile one for her and all the Jews.

I once heard someone say that favour is not fair—and I am inclined to agree. In my opinion, favour is the grace of God locating you, granting access to privileges you would not naturally receive or deserve. Esther found herself gaining the liking and privilege to enter spaces that would not have been afforded to her by natural means. She was an orphan, yet she became queen. She was a Jew, yet she was chosen above all the other Persian women. She was an outsider, yet she remained queen, even though the former queen was removed for simply protecting her dignity.

Favour will take you places you never dreamed of, and keep you in places you never even sought.

"Having favour is no small thing in a kingdom"

Knowing your value and your worth is important in your transformation process. Queen Esther understood her value and knew what worked for her. As a young girl under the guidance of her cousin Mordecai, she may not have fully grasped her worth. But as Queen Esther, with the fear of God and Mordecai's counsel, she matured into a woman who recognized her divine purpose. In the face of tragedy, she did not rush into action; instead, she prepared herself. She got dressed, presented herself intentionally, and approached the king with purpose.

Preparation makes a difference. It shows you are intentional, strategic, and purpose-driven. While Esther had already endured the tragedy of losing her parents, she now faced another one that threatened her entire nation.

As queen, she had to decide whether to risk her life by intervening for the Jews.

Esther understood that her royal position was not the pinnacle, it was a divine assignment.

Her crown was not simply an honour but a responsibility cloaked in purpose. She was called to be a transformational hero for her people.

When you truly understand who you are, you don't let the difficulty of your assignment dictate your response. You rise in boldness, knowing that there is more with you than against you. You face obstacles—be they physical, mental, emotional, or spiritual—head-on, trusting in the God who called you. Esther was willing to risk everything for her people. Her transformation became evident when she embraced her identity, overcame fear, and was fuelled by purpose. She was ready to declare who she truly was—a Jewish woman—despite the decree that Jews were to be killed.

"Just as the enemy plots your downfall, God is orchestrating your deliverance."

She knew the law: entering the king's court uninvited could mean death. Yet she moved forward. As transformed women, we must learn to do the same—trust God through the process and be willing to put it all on the line. Your destiny is in His hands. Just as the enemy plots your downfall, God is orchestrating your deliverance. It's time to tap into your true identity—as a daughter of the Most High God. He has your back, and He will never leave you alone.

So whatever you're facing today, face it boldly, knowing that God is with you, and you have what it takes.

"Go, gather together all the Jews that are
present in Shushan, and fast ye for me, and
neither eat nor drink three days, night or day:
I also and my maidens will fast
likewise; and so will I go in unto the king,
which is not according to the law:
and if I perish, I perish.

ESTHER 4 VS 16

Her Strategy

How a person chooses to respond to a situation can
have the greatest impact on its outcome. Esther was both
wise and strategic when she invited the king—along with
her adversary—to a banquet. She used her beauty and
patience not as manipulation, but as tools of engagement
to open the king's heart to conversation. Though she held
the royal title of queen, Esther understood that protocol
still mattered. She did not let her position make her
arrogant or forgetful of her role and responsibilities.

The strategy and wisdom were patience and humility.
Esther took the time she needed to prepare the heart of the
king to hear her request. In fact, the king became eager to
know what she desired, so much so that he offered her up
to half of the kingdom. Esther's strategy was not to rush
the process of their deliverance, even though it mattered
greatly.

What she needed was a favourable result.

And so, humility, patience, and wisdom became her divine
strategy.

As we grow through transformation, we too must be careful not to let our positions, titles, or blessings cloud our judgement. It is essential to recognize both our strengths and our limitations, because each can serve us in different ways. Being "right" does not always justify how we act or respond. True wisdom calls us to be mindful of our environment, sensitive to timing, and discerning in our approach.

Esther did not rely solely on her favour or appearance. She adapted to the Persian culture while remaining anchored in her identity as a woman of purpose. She approached the king with reverence, strategy, and discernment. In our journeys of transformation, we must learn to lean not just on our talents or charm, but on the God-given wisdom that leads us to act with grace, humility, and effectiveness.

> "Wisdom is the principle thing; therefore get wisdom: and with all thy getting get understanding."
>
> **PROVERBS 4 VS 7**

Esther knew she was loved and favoured by the king, but she also knew that she had God on her side—and if she was going to go before the king, she had to first go before the King of kings. As transformed women, we must know where our strength lies: our strength cometh from the Lord. God's hand was all over Esther's story, and He used her—under the guidance of her cousin Mordecai—to bring deliverance to an entire nation.

Esther did not rely solely on her beauty or the love of her husband. She trusted in God, asking all the Jews to fast and pray for three days. She embraced who she was and stepped fully into her position as queen. She faced her fear of going before the king without being summoned. Esther was transformed from a regular Jewish girl living in Persia to the Queen of Persia. Fittingly, the name Esther means star, and in Revelation 22:16, Jesus is called the "bright and morning star." Like Christ, who came to save the world, Esther walked boldly in the meaning of her name and in her divine calling, for such a time as this.

She walked in the anointing over her life, allowing Jehovah Nissi—the Lord our Banner—to use her as an instrument of salvation for her people. Her position in the kingdom of Persia was not about fame or popularity; she was on assignment. We, too, must show up and walk according to our kingdom mandate, not allowing titles, people, or worldly distractions to deter us. When we allow God to transform our lives, we can do more and be more, not just for ourselves, but for others as well.

Esther operated with wisdom, allowing God to lead her through prayer and fasting. Her obedience and strategic approach led the king to reverse the decree over the Jewish nation. Her discernment also resulted in Mordecai being elevated to a prominent role in the Persian kingdom, while their enemy Haman was hanged on the very gallows he had built for Mordecai.

"That is the reciprocity of transformation."

Know that you serve a God who, when you walk out your transformation, will not only lift you, but use your transformation to elevate others. I encourage you to walk in wisdom and be guided by the Spirit of the living God. There is nothing I desire more than to see lives transformed by the power of God. As He continues to transform me, I intentionally listen to His leading, which consistently calls me to help others through their own process, whether through one-on-one counselling, small group facilitation, prayer meetings, preaching, or teaching the Word. To know that someone's life is better—or inspired to become better—because of who I am and what I do is the ultimate reward. That is the reciprocity of transformation.

I can vividly remember, as a young girl just getting saved and filled with the Holy Spirit, spending time with God in personal devotion. Even at eleven years old, I prayed and asked God for wisdom. There have been many days and many moments in my life where God gave me wisdom to speak, even when I had no words. When I had no encouragement to share, He gave me the encouragement that was needed. God can endow you with wisdom that makes a difference in the lives of others.

I do not always know what to say or what to do, but God's wisdom has carried me through. It is for you to ask God for wisdom and the strategy to execute the plans He lays before you, as well as to avert the dangers the enemy may set in your path. As a parent, a wife, and even in my workplace, I have often had to go before the Lord in prayer, asking for guidance on what to do and how to navigate the situations before me.

Becoming Her Check-In

Reflect:
Have you ever felt placed somewhere on purpose, even if it felt uncomfortable or unfamiliar? How did you respond? What is your "for such a time as this" moment? Is there a calling, assignment, or bold step you've been avoiding? Have you ever had to advocate for someone else, even at a personal cost? How did that shape your identity?

Respond:
Ask God for the courage to walk in the assignment He has given you. Declare that you will not shrink back, but will step forward—clothed in prayer, wisdom, and divine favour.

Time of Meditation

Take a moment to meditate.
Reflect on who you are and identify areas in your life where you have experienced God's unprecedented favour. Consider who you are in Christ. Once you have done that, pause and begin to express your gratitude. Know that God's favour in your life not only positions you for transformation but also empowers you to become an agent of transformation.

Scriptures

———————◆———————

Esther 2:17
And the king loved Esther above all the women, and she obtained grace and favour in his sight more than all the virgins; so that he set the royal crown upon her head, and made her queen instead of Vashti.

Rev. 22:16
I Jesus have sent mine angel to testify unto you these things in the churches. I am the root and the offspring of David, and the bright and morning star.

1 Samuel 15:22
And Samuel said, Hath the Lord as great delight in burnt offerings and sacrifices, as in obeying the voice of the Lord? Behold, to obey is better than sacrifice, and to hearken than the fat of rams.

Proverbs 4:7
Wisdom is the principle thing; therefore get wisdom: and with all thy getting get understanding.

Psalm 139:14
I will praise thee; for I am fearfully and wonderfully made: marvelous are thy works; and that my soul knoweth right well.

Action Steps to
Transformation

Once you come to the realization of who you are, your purpose will begin to come alive within you. This is why it is essential to be self-aware of the spaces you can occupy in society and to seek God intentionally. Ask yourself: How can I show up in a way that brings change and transformation?

Begin by creating a list of real-life spaces you are connected to—your workplace, school, family, community, or social groups—and ask God how He can use you to bring transformation, not just for yourself, but for everyone in those spaces.

_____

_____

_____

_____

_____

_____

_____

_____

_____

_____

Action Steps to
Transformation

In life, character matters, and Esther used wisdom as a key characteristic in how she proceeded to bring forth change in and around her. Are there moments in past situations where you can now recognize that, had you used wisdom, the outcome may have been better? If yes, take time to identify one or two of those moments with a renewed mindset, not to dwell in regret, but to grow. Reflect on how you can approach similar situations differently moving forward, without allowing a spirit of condemnation to set in.

_____

_____

_____

_____

_____

_____

_____

_____

_____

_____

Action Steps to
Transformation

As a transformed woman of God, you are now aware that who you are, how you live your life, and the choices you make should have an impact on those in your circle. So now, what are some intentional steps or choices you can make to show up differently for those around you, whether it be your family, friends, or colleagues?

_____

_____

_____

_____

_____

_____

_____

_____

_____

_____

_____

_____

A
PRAYER
For You!

Heavenly Father,
I present my sister before you as she engages in
her process of transformation. I ask that you
position her—in life, in society, and within her
family—in such a way that she will not only
influence high places but also bring about change
and transformation that will impact lives.
Help her to recognize her gifts, her value, and her
worth, so that you may use her and place her in
unimaginable spaces to elevate others and bring
about significant change.
Grace her with godly wisdom to guide her
decisions and govern her responses in every
situation. Let her know that you are with her, as
her King and her Lord, and that you will never
leave her, even when the process becomes
difficult.
Remind her that with you, all things are possible.
Let her see clearly that where she begins is not
where she will end. All she needs to do, just like
Esther, is walk in obedience and trust you with
everything she faces in life.
In Jesus' name, Amen.

Positioning

Key Takeaways

Transformation

✔ Know your value and your self-worth!

✔ Do not allow tragedy to deter you from your purpose.

✔ Function with Godly wisdom

―――――――

Becoming Her: Courage

Esther, cloaked in courage, stepped into the court not just as queen, but as a deliverer—becoming her for such a time as this.

notes

Abigail

Transformed to Save lives and Preserve Destiny

~~~~~

Abigail understood who she was, hence allowing her to act quickly, which saved the lives of her household and preserved the destiny of King David.

The wife of a fool

I want to introduce you to this brave woman in the Bible whose name is Abigail (1 Samuel 25). She was married to Nabal, a man described as rich, very wealthy, but also arrogant and harsh. If we want to be more specific, Nabal's name means "fool." This is important information because it shows us how Abigail rose to the occasion and became a transformed woman by intervening to save her foolish husband.

Beyond saving her husband, she was monumental in preventing the future king from reacting harshly to the conduct of a foolish man by taking vengeance into his own hands. On the other hand, Abigail was described as both understanding and beautiful. She was an extraordinary woman who was far more than her beauty, compassionate, generous, and intelligent. She became a destiny helper to many. She was able to help others, but unfortunately, unlike her foolish husband, not everyone accepted her help.

This demonstrates that while we may desire to assist many, not all will accept our assistance. As transformed women, we may carry the desire to bring many along with us, but we must discern the individuals we are assigned to help. Never be afraid to move forward because of those who refuse your help. And never carry the guilt of their unwillingness to receive it."

The need to intervene

It all began when David sent men to request food from Nabal, a rich and able man in the community. David chose Nabal not only because he could afford it—which he certainly could—but also because David and his men had willingly protected Nabal's workers from the Philistines while they were in the field during the sheep-shearing season. David had done this voluntarily, without any request from Nabal.

Rather than responding with kindness and generosity, Nabal answered arrogantly. He refused even to acknowledge who David was, denying compensation to David and his men for the protection they had offered. He went as far as insinuating that David was a runaway—an insult not only to the future king but also a direct reflection of Nabal's foolish character.

Nabal's insult and contemptuous behaviour were not well received by David. In response, David gathered some of his men with the intent to wipe out Nabal and his entire household. The scriptures reveal this intention clearly. Everyone who knew David, the warrior king, understood he was more than capable of wiping out Nabal's entire community. Nabal's foolish actions left his family and servants vulnerable, which is why Abigail had to leave her daily duties and run out to intervene on behalf of her husband and household.

The moment the servant made Abigail aware of David's intention, she sprang into action. As transformed women, we need to know when and how to intervene. It is our responsibility to intercede on our family's behalf. It is our job to advocate, pray, and encourage our families, friends, and loved ones.

Her character is her gift

The wonderful thing about Abigail's story is that she truly understood people. She was a woman of great discernment, and it was this gift that prompted her to act quickly and save her household from David's wrath. In doing so, she also saved David from stepping outside of God's will for his life. Above all, Abigail understood who she was and the gifts she possessed. This self-awareness enabled her to intervene—not just to save her own life and household, but even her husband, who had acted out of arrogance.

Abigail was quick-witted and responded without delay once she learned of David's intentions. She didn't waste time, knowing that David, a seasoned warrior, was fully capable of destroying their entire household because of her husband's poor judgment. Without consulting or debating with her husband, she prepared what she believed would satisfy David and his men. Her discernment told her that swift, decisive action was necessary.

Another characteristic Abigail demonstrated was humility. As she approached David, she bowed and honoured him. She used wisdom to intervene, redirecting David back to his purpose and encouraging him not to act out of vengeance in response to her husband's ignorance. Knowing that David had been chosen by God to be king, she urged him to remain aligned with God's will rather than be led by anger.

A transformed woman understands her gifts and uses them to support others on their God-given path to destiny. She is not manipulative or self-serving. Abigail did not seek to save herself alone—she stood in the gap for her entire household. She didn't lie or manipulate the situation; instead, she acknowledged her husband's foolishness and took accountability on his behalf. A transformed woman—especially one who is a wife—stands for righteousness.

It was not a moment to make excuses or act in ignorance; Abigail was called to stand for what was right while interceding on behalf of others. She placed herself between David and her husband, courageously bridging the gap. As a wife, I've experienced many moments where I, too, had to stand in the gap and intercede for my husband—and now, for my children. We must understand the weight of our role and not delay when it is time to intervene for our loved ones, especially when trouble is near.

Is it not remarkable that the servant chose to inform Abigail and not Nabal? Perhaps it was because she had consistently demonstrated wisdom, compassion, and sound judgment. Her character had left a lasting impression on those around her, so much so that they trusted her to intervene. Her reputation for discernment and humility was clearly well known within her household.

"A transformed woman can understand her gift and use it to help others in their god given path to their destiny."

***

Becoming his wife

The beauty of Abigail's story is that she remained true to who she was, consistently operating in the gifts and calling placed on her life. It didn't matter who she was married to or who was in her presence—she acted with integrity and aligned herself with purpose. Her consistency and character were so profound that David, the future king, took notice of her. When he later heard that her husband had died, he sent for her and made her his wife. It is safe to say that Abigail did not begin her journey imagining that she would one day become queen.

Yet, by simply walking in the light of her identity, her character shone so brightly that it positioned her for elevation.

We must learn to see ourselves the way God sees us and recognize that the gifts He has placed within us are designed to make a difference. We carry the potential to influence others and be elevated in the kingdom of God, not for our own gain, but to serve a greater purpose. Who we are and the qualities we possess are not just personal strengths; they are divine tools to be used for God's glory. Abigail's God-given characteristics allowed her to become a destiny helper—not only for David, the future king, but also for her household and the servants who trusted her with critical information.

"It is my responsibility to walk out my salvation with confidence, knowing that God has called me and anointed me."

Over the years, I have come to understand that who I am is an asset, even if others fail to recognize it. It is my responsibility to walk out my salvation with confidence, knowing that God has called and anointed me. I must walk in the authority He has given me and refuse to conform to others' perceptions. By embracing my God-given identity, I can become more authentic, trustworthy, and effective in serving and ministering to those He has assigned to my care.

Becoming Her Check- In

> **Reflect:**
> *Take a moment to reflect on how you show up in the lives of others.*
> *Abigail used wisdom, humility, and discernment to step into a difficult situation and shift the outcome.*
> - *Where can I use my discernment more intentionally in my relationships?*
> - *Who has God called me to intercede or advocate for in this season?*
> - *How can I lead with grace, even when surrounded by chaos?*
>
> *Remember:*
> *Becoming her means walking in your God-given wisdom—even when it's uncomfortable—and trusting that your character will always make room for your calling.*

Time of Meditation

Let us take a moment to meditate on how our characteristics can be used to be a blessing in our daily lives. Who we are is not a detriment, but rather an asset to us and to those whom God has entrusted to us. Abigail's servant trusted her with pertinent information that ultimately saved their lives. Abigail practiced using wisdom rather than leaning into her husband's foolish characteristics. When we embrace who God has created us to be and choose to walk in that identity with intention, it can lead us to a truly transformed life.

Scriptures

❖

Genesis 1:27
So God created man in his own image, in the image of God created he him; male and female created he them.

Proverbs 4:7
Wisdom is the principal thing; therefore get wisdom: and with all thy getting get understanding.

Proverbs 9:10
The fear of the Lord is the beginning of wisdom: and the knowledge of the holy is understanding.

Proverb 9:13
A foolish woman is clamorous: she is simple, and knoweth nothing.

Proverbs 16:16
much better is it to get wisdom than gold! and to get understanding rather to be chosen than silver!

Hebrew 5:14
But strong meat belongeth to them that are of full age, even those who by reason of use have their senses exercised to discern both good and evil.

Action Steps to Transformation

Now, with the understanding that God has created each of us intentionally and lovingly, just as we are, I invite you to pause and reflect: Who are you at your core? What are the unique characteristics that God has woven into your being? Take a moment to consider the qualities that best describe you. Are you compassionate? Resilient? Joyful? A seeker of truth? A peacemaker?

As you reflect, remember that these traits—both your strengths and your areas for growth—are part of the beautiful and intentional design God has placed within you. Embrace them with gratitude, knowing they reflect His handiwork in your life.

_____

_____

_____

_____

_____

_____

_____

_____

_____

Action Steps to
Transformation

As a transformed woman, being self-aware of who you are is essential. Just like Abigail, who had trusted individuals in her life who could recognize her positive characteristics, I encourage you to identify a few close friends and ask them for honest feedback. Invite them to describe your character—how they see you, what stands out about you, and what strengths they believe you consistently demonstrate.

_____

_____

_____

_____

_____

_____

_____

_____

_____

_____

_____

Action Steps to
Transformation

No doubt that Abigail was consistent in who she was and how she lived her life as a woman of
God. You and I are on a journey to live a transformed life. Do you believe that you have lived a
consistent lifestyle that demonstrates Godly characteristics? And if not, what can you do to change that, and if yes, put to words how you have been consistent?

_____

_____

_____

_____

_____

_____

_____

_____

_____

_____

_____

A
PRAYER
For You!

As I approach the throne of grace, I ask that my sister would seek a deeper understanding of who she is in You. May she acknowledge that she is made in the image of God—reflecting Your nature and character—and fully embrace every godly trait You have placed within her. I pray that You give her the courage to become and to do all that You have willed for her life. Let her walk in consistency and live out a transformed life, ready to take action, to intervene, and to intercede for those You have called her to support.

Lord, my prayer is that You bring her through the process of transformation. Mould her character so that she becomes pleasant, loving, kind, gentle, discerning, and full of wisdom. May she become the kind of woman others are drawn to—attracting the right people and making wise decisions—so she may be positioned to transform the lives of others. Help her, Lord, to continually acknowledge who You have created her to be. Let her desire to honour You with her life—by being authentic in everything she does and everywhere she goes.

Thank You for trusting her
with Your gifts.
Amen.

Authenticity

Key Takeaways

Transformation

✓ Have a trustworthy character

✓ Be bold and know that you possess what it takes to intervene on behalf of others

✓ You are someone's destiny helper.

Becoming Her: Discernment

Abigail, led by discernment, moved with grace and wisdom, becoming her in the moment that mattered most.

notes

Zipporah

Transformed into a New Covenant

Zipporah was a woman from a different nation, but by becoming Moses' wife, she entered into a new covenant that transformed her life. Her obedience played a pivotal role in preserving the life of a great leader.

The Meditation Wife

Zipporah was a Midianite, the daughter of Jethro, a priest of Midian. Moses met her after fleeing Egypt for killing an Egyptian. In Midian, Moses encountered Zipporah and her sisters at a well and, like a true protector, he rescued them from shepherds who tried to drive them away while drawing water for their flock. That moment marked a divine intersection of life and purpose. Zipporah later became Moses' wife, a Midianite woman who joined in covenant with a Hebrew man. This union required them to learn and respect each other's cultures, a significant detail as her story unfolds.

We see Zipporah as a devoted wife who gave space for her husband to grow into the leader he was called to be. She embraced his faith and entered into covenant by honouring his religious practices. In doing so, she ensured those practices were upheld, even when Moses himself hesitated.

71

It was in her obedience and spiritual awareness that her transformation became evident. Zipporah embodies the truth behind the saying, "Behind every great man is a great woman."

As transformed women, we are reminded through her life that regardless of the personal or cultural differences we may encounter in marriage, we are called to remain anchored in our role and responsibilities—being the best helpmate we can be, led by the Word of God and the guidance of the Holy Spirit.

"Behind every great man is a great woman"

His Mandate, Her Mandate

When Moses was called and mandated to lead the Israelites out of Egypt, he entered into covenant with God. As a result, he was required to follow God's laws as an example to the people he would lead. Moses' failure to circumcise his sons was a significant oversight, as circumcision was not optional—it was a covenantal law established in Genesis 17:10. As God's appointed representative to the Israelites, Moses was expected to fully walk in obedience and model the laws he would soon be teaching to others. His disobedience revealed a disconnect between the covenant he was called to uphold and his personal actions. Although scripture does not detail a direct conversation between God and Zipporah, as Moses' wife and helpmate, she played a critical role in supporting his divine mandate.

Her responsibility was not only to stand beside him but also to ensure she did not hinder the fulfilment of his calling.

Moses' neglect to circumcise their son became a life-or-death matter. As they journeyed together in obedience to God's call, the Lord sought to kill Moses for this act of disobedience. Whether it was out of deep love, conviction, or spiritual discernment, Zipporah stepped in. She took a flint knife and circumcised their son, intervening in a moment that required swift, decisive action. Her obedience saved Moses' life (Exodus 4:24-26).

This moment marks Zipporah's transformation, from a woman of a different cultural background into a devoted wife aligned with God's covenant. She did not allow her upbringing or personal tradition to block her from responding to God's will. As transformed women, we too must resist conforming to the familiar or the comfortable. Instead, we are called to be transformed, to align with God's will and act boldly when the moment demands it. Zipporah's act was more than tradition; it was obedience that preserved a destiny.

"Zipporah was not Jewish by birth, yet her action demonstrated her faith in and belief in the God of Moses."

A Devoted Wife

Though Zipporah was not Jewish by birth, her actions demonstrated her faith in and belief in the God of Moses. Zipporah was a woman of deep loyalty, dedication, strength, and humility.

Her profound understanding of the weight and responsibility her husband carried is evident in the scriptures, and I believe it was this awareness that motivated her to respond the way she did.

Despite their cultural differences, Zipporah recognized who her husband was and rose to intervene, ultimately saving Moses's life. This was a powerful act of support. She chose to be a helpmate rather than confront him or highlight his failure. Instead, she stood in the gap, acting swiftly by circumcising their son. She operated in Moses' stead, a clear demonstration of their unity—becoming one in purpose and covenant.

Culturally, the act of circumcision was not a woman's responsibility. Yet her bold and immediate intervention brought life, as God spared Moses. In that moment of courageous obedience, Zipporah set the stage for Moses to walk fully in his calling as a great leader.

Their relationship was marked by blood and covenant, symbolized in her words, "A bloody husband thou art, because of the circumcision"(Exodus 4:26). This was more than a cultural act—it was the action of a devoted woman whose heart had been transformed. Her devotion transcended cultural and religious boundaries, signifying her personal alignment with the God of Israel and the covenant her husband carried.

Wife to the greatest leader

Every woman who desires to marry a husband of greatness must be prepared to support that greatness, regardless of how it is initially packaged. In becoming her —a wife to a man of divine purpose—we must understand our role and not allow personal needs or emotions to hinder what God is doing in our presence.

We are called to fill the gaps God assigns us and to carry out the unexpected tasks He sets before us. Our acts of obedience, as transformed women, have the power to preserve lives.

Moses was appointed to lead a nation. Zipporah recognized the calling and mandate on his life and made critical decisions that helped him become one of the greatest leaders of Israel—a monumental biblical figure honoured across generations. Had she not responded in obedience and discernment, Moses's life would have been forfeited.

Someone within your circle—your family, community, or church—is waiting for your act of obedience. God is calling you to stand in the gap and help birth others into their destiny. It is our responsibility to support our husbands in their calling and ensure that our families are following the precepts of God's Word.

Zipporah married Moses the shepherd, but through transformation, by embracing his people and his God, she emerged as the wife of one of the greatest leaders in history.

On my journey of transformation, it is my obedience to God's Word and leadership that is shaping me into the leader and wife He has called me to be. The fruit of that obedience is shown in how I support my husband, choosing not to criticize his weaknesses, but to cover him in prayer. I've even created a dedicated room in our home where he can pray and grow spiritually.

I do my best not to override his leadership in our home, though I'm still learning! When I'm home, I choose to function as Dejah, not by my title. I intentionally recognize and live out the role of a helpmate, understanding that there will be times I must lead certain initiatives, not for my ego, but for the benefit of our family.

As a transformed woman, following my God-given mandate doesn't exempt me from my calling as a godly wife. In becoming her, we are called to intercede and intercept the plans of the enemy. We stand in the gap to protect the destiny, dreams, and vision of those we are assigned to love.

Becoming Her Check-In

Reflect:

Take a quiet moment to reflect on your role as a support, a partner, and a vessel of obedience.

- *Where in your life has God called you to stand in the gap for someone else?*
- *Are there areas where your swift obedience could preserve or push someone toward their destiny?*
- *In what ways have you embraced transformation to walk beside the people God has assigned to you?*
- *Are you honouring the spiritual mandate over your household with prayer, intercession, and grace?*

Pray:

Ask God to give you a heart that discerns, a spirit that obeys, and hands willing to act. Your obedience may be the key that unlocks someone else's calling.

Time of Meditation

Zipporah is such an inspirational biblical character. During this time of meditation, I invite you to reflect on your understanding of the mandate placed on your God-given spouse. How you proceed in helping him walk out that mandate matters. Marriage is a covenant, not to be broken, dismissed, or taken lightly. Let the Word of God be your guide in this transformation journey, shaping you into the kind of wife who knows how and when to intervene and intercede with wisdom, grace, and divine timing.

Scriptures

---❖---

Genesis 17:

10 This is my covenant, which ye shall keep, between me and you and thy seed after thee; Every man child among you shall be circumcised.
11 And ye shall circumcise the flesh of your foreskin; and it shall be a token of the covenant betwixt me and you.
12 And he that is eight days old shall be circumcised among you, every man child in your
generations, he that is born in the house, or bought with money of any stranger, which is not of thy seed.
13 He that is born in thy house, and he that is bought with thy money, must needs be circumcised:
and my covenant shall be in your flesh for an everlasting covenant.
14 And the uncircumcised man child whose flesh of his foreskin is not circumcised, that soul shall be cut off from his people; he hath broken my covenant.

1 Samuel 15: 22

And Samuel said, Hath the Lord as great delight in burnt offerings and sacrifices, as in obeying the
voice of the Lord? Behold, to obey is better than sacrifice, and to hearken than the fat of rams.

Action Steps to Transformation

As transformed women, we are called to walk in obedience to God. Obedience is not always easy, but it is essential—because our choices carry weight, and our obedience can lead to powerful, even eternal, outcomes.

Take a moment to reflect: Have there been times when you ignored God's voice or His clear direction, even if it seemed like you were helping someone else? Sometimes what feels like kindness or sacrifice can actually be disobedience in disguise. Now that you recognize where you may have gone off course, don't dwell in regret. Instead, choose growth. Let this awareness lead you to take intentional steps toward change, so that moving forward, your obedience aligns fully with God's will. Remember, God's grace is sufficient, and His Spirit will guide you as you commit to walking in truth and purpose.

_____

_____

_____

_____

_____

_____

_____

Action Steps to
Transformation

Our lack of obedience to God's directives can lead to serious consequences. Take some time to search the Scriptures and list two or three examples where disobedience to God resulted in significant consequences. What lessons can you draw from those stories that apply to your walk with God?

_____

_____

_____

_____

_____

_____

_____

_____

_____

_____

_____

Action Steps to
Transformation

Zipporah did not ignore who she was; rather, she embraced her husband's tradition. With her loving and caring nature, she was able to use her God-given gifts to make a difference. Each of us has been blessed with the ability to help others.
Take a moment to reflect:
What are some of the characteristics or gifts you possess that can be used right now to help someone in your life?

_____

_____

_____

_____

_____

_____

_____

_____

_____

_____

_____

A
PRAYER
For You!

Oh Lord,
I give You thanks for Your favour and the calling You've placed on our lives. I pray that You would grant us the strength to walk in obedience and live lives that are pleasing to You. Help us to surrender our will and yield to Yours alone.

We desire to honour You and be a help to others. Use us, Lord—send us to the people You have assigned us to support. As You transform us, we are open and willing to be conduits for transformation in the lives of others.

I pray that as You lead us, I will choose the path of obedience and be a guide for my family. In following Your will, I long to become the best version of myself. Help us to honour those You have placed in leadership before us, and not become hindrances, but rather vessels of value, love, and support. We ask all of this in Your precious name, Jesus.
Amen.

Obedience

Key Takeaways

Transformation

✓ Understand your role as a wife

✓ Identify the mandate of your spouse

✓ As a transformed woman, your identity is in Christ, not your culture

---

Becoming Her: Faithful

Zipporah, faithful in love and fierce in purpose, became her by stepping beyond custom and comfort—covering destiny in quiet strength.

notes

Sarah

Transformed from My Will to God's will.

~~~

Sarah struggled for years with infertility. Though God had promised her and her husband a son, she chose to resolve the problem in a traditional way, rather than waiting on God's will to unfold.

Transformed through a Name change

One of the first processes of transformation that God led Sarah through was a name change. In Genesis 17:15, we see God informing her husband that she would no longer be called Sarai, but Sarah. While this transformation of name isn't explained in great detail, it signifies that because God had chosen Abraham, his wife was also included in the Abrahamic covenant. Being part of that covenant afforded Sarah the blessing of becoming the mother of nations and bearing the promised son.

"And God said unto Abraham, As for Sarai, thy wife, thou shalt not call her name Sarai, but Sarah shall her name be."

GENESIS 17:15

Transformation through a miracle

Many of us know the story of Sarah as the woman through whom God performed the miracle of childbirth long after she had passed the age of childbearing. This was not just a miracle—it was the fulfilment of a promise. Sarah went through many stages of transformation, which are recorded throughout the book of Genesis.

Although not the first, this particular moment was among the most significant. Sarah was barren and had no children of her own. Knowing that God had promised her husband that he would have children—and that the promised child would come through her—one can only imagine the desperation Sarah must have felt year after year, wondering how such a promise could ever come to pass.

"Sarah could not walk on the same level of faith, she carried in her early years."

Through this process, Sarah's transformation was not accidental; it was intentional and divinely orchestrated. She was now a part of a greater plan, one that extended beyond her identity as Abraham's wife. Sarah was being positioned for queen status: to become the mother of a nation, a chosen nation. To step into this promise, Sarah could no longer operate with the same level of faith she had in her earlier years. At ninety years old, God challenged her to believe for a child—a miracle in a season that most would deem impossible. As transformed women, we must elevate our faith to match where God is taking us, the people He is calling us to, and the assignments He will require us to carry out. He is calling us to a greater dimension of faith.

This growth process will stretch us, confront us with unfamiliar challenges, and demand belief in the unseen. Sarah may not have known how or when it would happen, but she held onto what God had spoken. She understood that it would require a miracle and unwavering faith to see the promised child come to pass.

In her natural reasoning, she couldn't comprehend the possibility. But a transformed mind understands that with God, all things are possible. And if God said it, then there must be a way for it to happen.

As transformed women, we must elevate our faith to match where God is taking us, the people He is calling us to, and the things He will require of us to accomplish. God will stretch us to transform our faith into a greater faith.

In our growth process, we will be challenged by things we have never seen or experienced before. Sarah may not have known how or when, exactly—but she knew God had said it. And she knew it would take both a miracle and unwavering faith to see the promised child come to fruition.

Sarah, in her own flesh, could not see the possibility. But a transformed mind knows that all things are possible with God, and if God said it, then there must be a way for it to happen.

Transformed by a mistake

I do not know about you, but one of my learning tools —though unfortunate at times—is learning from my mistakes. Making mistakes often provides us with the opportunity to learn and grow. Sarah had to learn a hard lesson from one prominent mistake she made.

This mistake was driven by her fear of not seeing God's promise fulfilled due to her physical state of barrenness and the limitation of her age, as noted in Genesis 11.

As transformed women, we cannot allow our physical limitations or worldly mindsets to limit what God can do in our lives. It is our responsibility to wait on the Lord, no matter how long it takes or how impossible it seems. Yes, in the natural and from a worldly perspective, it was an impossible situation—but with God, a barren woman well past childbearing age can conceive. God is a God who specializes in impossibilities!

It is not enough for us to merely recite the Word of God; we must allow our minds to be transformed by the Word until it becomes our reality. Sarah chose to assist God by having her servant Hagar become a surrogate for her and Abraham. This decision disrupted their household and was not in alignment with God's will. Hagar conceived and, in turn, became arrogant and provocative toward Sarah (Genesis 16:4).

> "And he went in unto Hagar, and she conceived: and when she saw that she had conceived, her mistress was despised in her eyes."
>
> GENESIS 16:4

Though this was customary, not everything that is customary is approved by God. God's Word will never fall to the ground, and if He said that a barren woman over 90 years old would have a promised child, then that is what it is. Though Hagar gave Abraham his first son, Ishmael, he was not the promised child. This mistake taught Sarah a transformative lesson: God does not need our help. Time and physical limitations are no match for the power of God. Sarah learned that God is not limited by time or season; all she needed was faith in His Word and His promise while she waited for its fulfillment.

One thing I have discovered during my walk with Christ is that transformation is a process, and it is continuous. Like Sarah, during my waiting period for the child God told me would come, there were moments I wanted to give up because of my human limitations.

I, too, entertained the thought of adoption, thinking maybe that would be the means through which God's promise would be fulfilled in our lives. The desperate desire to meet my need and experience the fulfillment of God's promise was so intense that I explored every possible option.

I had to get to a place where my faith surpassed my fear.

Transformed through confrontation

Sarah's submission to God's will—despite her laughter —was where her full transformation took place. The Angel of the Lord prophesied that this time next year, Sarah would be with child. Sarah laughed in disbelief, but when confronted with the truth, her heart submitted to God's will for her life. We need to be honest about where we are.

Hiding how we feel and what is going on in our hearts and minds is not worth sacrificing our blessings. God knows the heart. This is what He judges—not our outward appearances or mere verbal utterances. He looks at the authenticity of who we are.

Sarah's transformation allowed her to walk out her destiny and become the mother of a nation. Sarah's destiny was in God's hands—and so is yours. God is the author of your faith, and nothing about you is hidden from Him. He will lead you if you are willing to be submissive to His will and not follow your own way. Through your transformation, seek to know God's plan for your life, because how you start is not how you will finish. Sarah started as Sarai, the wife of Abram, and became Sarah, the wife of Abraham. She began barren but ended up as the mother of nations. Where you start is not where you will end.

Transformation brings change—not only in your life but in the lives of others. Like Sarah, I may not have had a name change, but I, too, was considered barren. Yet, through the process of time, with much prayer and supplication, my life was transformed with two beautiful children.

There is a blessing awaiting you in your process of becoming her—the new you, the non-barren, fruitful you.

Becoming Her Check-In

Reflect:

As you reflect on Sarah's journey, take a moment to consider your own:

- Where in your life have you allowed fear or impatience to guide your decisions instead of faith?
- Are there promises from God that you have nearly given up on because of how impossible they seem?
- In what areas is God inviting you to grow from doubt to belief, from barrenness to fruitfulness?

Sarah's story reminds us that delay is not denial. Transformation often takes time, but God is faithful to complete what He started. Just as Sarah's name and destiny were changed, your story is also being rewritten by His hand.

Pause & Ask Yourself;

What do I need to surrender so my faith can grow stronger than my fear? Am I willing to trust God's timing over my own understanding? Transformation begins the moment we stop striving and start believing.

Time of Meditation

Let us take a moment and meditate on the Word of God and how we can be transformed by faith during our waiting period. It is the Word that renews our minds and strengthens our faith—this must become our daily practice. God can use anyone, anything, and any moment to carry us through our process of transformation. Stay rooted in His Word, for it is in the waiting that your faith is refined and your promise begins to unfold.

Scriptures

---❖---

Isaiah 40: 31
But they that wait upon the LORD shall renew their strength; they shall mount up with wings
as eagles; they shall run, and not be weary; and they shall walk, and not faint.

Romans 10:17
So then faith cometh by hearing, and hearing by the word of God.

Hebrew 11:1
Now faith is the substance of things hoped for, the evidence of things not seen.

Number 23:19
God is not a man, that he should lie; neither the son of man, that he should repent: hath he
said, and shall he not do it? or hath he spoken, and shall he not make it good?

Action Steps to
Transformation

Have you taken the time to seek God regarding who you are and where He is taking you?
 If not, today is a good time to begin.
 Start by praying—ask God to reveal your identity and His plans for your life.
Then, take time to sit quietly and write down the thoughts, scriptures, or impressions you receive
Be patient. God speaks in His time and His way.
Trust that He desires to show you who you are becoming in Him.

_____

_____

_____

_____

_____

_____

_____

_____

_____

_____

Action Steps to
Transformation

Exercising faith is not always as easy as it may seem.
Take a moment to reflect on your life and recognize the patterns where you've struggled to walk by faith.
Be honest with yourself—acknowledging the areas of fear, doubt, or control is the first step to change.
Now, begin to identify specific action steps you can take to elevate your faith walk.
Write them down.
Then, invite the Holy Spirit to guide you through each one, covering your heart in prayer and anchoring your mind in daily meditation on the Word.

Action Steps to Transformation

One of the things that has always helped me is consulting not only with the Holy Spirit but also with those trusted individuals whom God has placed in my life—people who pray for me, guide me, and speak truth into my spirit.

Alongside seeking God, seek wise counsel from those in your spiritual circle. Take time to identify who they are. Now, write down the words of wisdom, encouragement, or correction they've shared with you to strengthen your faith walk. Let these trusted voices become anchors as you continue your journey of transformation.

_____

_____

_____

_____

_____

_____

_____

_____

_____

_____

_____

A
PRAYER
For You!

Dear Heavenly Father,
I know that You have a plan for our
lives, and we desire to live out that
plan. We humbly come to You, seeking
Your wisdom, guidance, and revelation
concerning what those plans are and
what they look like.
Lord, we ask that You send the right
people into our lives—those who will
uplift and strengthen us as we walk by
faith toward our destiny in this process
of transformation.
Help us, O God, to submit to Your will
for our lives and to be patient through
it all. We ask for the grace to move
beyond our past mistakes and allow
them to bring growth and
transformation.
In Jesus' name,
Amen.

Guidance

Key Takeaways

Transformation

✔ Faith is pivotal to our transformation

✔ Your mistakes do not define you, but it is an opportunity for change

✔ Submit yourself to the will of God

Becoming Her: Hope

Sarah, worn by waiting but lifted by God's word, held onto the whisper of the unseen, becoming her in the unshakeable light of hope.

notes

Rebekah

Transformed by Faith by Unorthodox Means

A woman of faith and strong belief in the God of her forefathers, Rebekah moved beyond inherited familiarity to a personal encounter with God. Through an unorthodox means, she witnessed the unfolding of God's word and the fulfillment of divine promise.

The answered Prayer and The Woman of Destiny

When Rebekah first enters the biblical narrative, she is introduced as a young woman marked by obedience, confidence, compassion, and unwavering faith. Her story begins during a focal moment in history, when Abraham's trusted servant was sent to find a wife for Isaac, the promised son and heir to Abraham's covenant with God. This task was not taken lightly. The servant was given clear instructions, fully aware that Isaac's wife would be more than just a partner; she would be a matriarch, a pillar, a spiritual leader alongside Isaac as he carried forth the legacy of Abraham and the future of a nation.

This woman could not be ordinary. She had to be strong in character, spiritually attuned, and bold in faith.

So, with a heart set on fulfilling his mission faithfully, the servant prayed. He asked God for a specific sign to identify the right woman—someone whose actions would reveal her heart. And God, in His divine instrumentation, answered with Rebekah. She didn't come with fanfare or grand gestures. She simply showed up: faithful, humble, and ready to serve. At the well, Rebekah went out of her way to draw water not just for the servant but also for his camels, a tiring and time-consuming task. Yet, she did it without complaint. In that moment, her character spoke louder than words. She was kind, patient, hardworking, and hospitable. She didn't see the task as beneath her or burdensome. What others might have considered menial, she embraced with grace. This small act of service revealed the depth of who she was: a woman of strength, humility, and quiet dignity.

Rebekah wasn't just chosen by the servant; she was chosen by God. She was an answer to prayer. A divine selection. The kind of woman who didn't just meet expectations, she exceeded them by embodying the very qualities that would make her a mother of nations.
Let her introduction remind us:

Sometimes the greatest doors open through simple acts of obedience.

Sometimes God's chosen are revealed through their willingness to serve, not to be seen.

And sometimes, the most powerful beginnings are wrapped in humility.

Twenty Years of Barrenness

Though Rebekah was divinely chosen to be Isaac's wife, she faced a painful and disheartening trial: infertility. Like many women in her position, Rebekah was deeply distraught.

99

But what makes this part of her story especially powerful is the role her husband played. Isaac didn't give up. Instead, he earnestly and persistently sought God in prayer on her behalf. Even when hope seemed distant and they faced the ridicule of delay, Isaac remained steadfast, interceding on behalf of his wife.

"Even in seasons of silence, faith and support can carry us forward."

Many of us face circumstances that tempt us to give in to fear or to turn away from the presence of God. But Rebekah held her ground, supported by a husband who prayed her through her pain. Her story is a reminder that even in seasons of silence, faith and support can carry us forward.

One night, while asleep, Rebekah had a dream—a divine reassurance from God Himself that she would become a mother. Imagine the joy and peace that must have filled her heart. After years of waiting, God had spoken—and once God speaks, His word cannot return void.

Not long after, Rebekah conceived. But this wasn't an easy pregnancy. She experienced turmoil and discomfort beyond the usual. Once again, God had spoken—this time to reveal that she was carrying twins, and more importantly, that two nations were within her womb. He told her that the older would serve the younger, a revelation that went against the customs of the time but aligned perfectly with God's sovereign plan. Rebekah understood something that others around her couldn't. She carried a promise—one that was not just about children but about destiny, legacy, and nations. Sometimes, no one else will understand what you carry.

But when God speaks a word into your life, it is your responsibility to guard that word, hold it close, protect it from doubt, and believe in its fulfillment.

"Your transformation begins with a word—and that word and that word can come straight from the throne of God to your spirit."

———————————

Rebekah clung to that prophetic word. Even when the culture, the tradition, and even her husband pointed in a different direction, she remembered what God had said. Her story reminds us that even amid struggle, we can hear God's voice clearly. We don't have to wait for a prophet, pastor, or teacher to validate what God has already spoken. He speaks directly to those who seek Him. Your transformation begins with a word, and that word can come straight from the throne of God to your spirit. It is crucial that we position ourselves in God's presence, surrounding ourselves with the right people—those who will pray with us, uplift us, and not plant seeds of doubt. In those sacred spaces, we are best able to hear God's direction, hold on to His promises, and walk faithfully into our calling.

From Wife to Matriarch

Rebekah's story is a profound example of how God's promises can be fulfilled in unexpected and unorthodox ways.

She was the wife of Isaac, a faithful man of God, determined to carry forward the legacy and promise God had given to his father, Abraham. Together, they had two sons, Esau and Jacob. According to tradition, the birthright and the father's blessing were meant for the firstborn, Esau. But Rebekah had heard something different from God. She knew in her heart what God had spoken. She sensed that Jacob, the younger son, was the one chosen to carry the blessing. Yet, Isaac seemed determined to follow the customs of the time. Faced with this tension, Rebekah took matters into her own hands. She devised a plan to ensure that Jacob received the blessing instead of Esau, just as she believed God had revealed it to her.

"Even amid confusion, conflict, and questionable decisions, God's will can still prevail."

To many, her actions may seem deceptive or even manipulative. Certainly, they were unorthodox. They might appear unbecoming of the woman who would become the matriarch of Israel, the chosen nation, set apart by God. Yet this story powerfully illustrates that even amid confusion, conflict, and questionable decisions, God's will can still prevail.

Rebekah's intervention altered the course of history. Jacob, not Esau, received the blessing and became the father of the twelve tribes of Israel. What began as a mother's controversial choice became the foundation of a nation. Rebekah was no longer just Isaac's wife; she was the foremother of God's chosen people.

But there's also a caution in her story. Though the promise was fulfilled, the method came with consequences —division, deception, and years of separation between brothers. It reminds us that obedience is better than sacrifice and that God is sovereign, more than capable of fulfilling His word without our interference.

Let Rebekah's story encourage you today: position yourself to hear from God. Seek Him in your times of uncertainty. Trust His timing, His process, and His power. If He has made you a promise, He will bring it to pass. Our role is to walk in obedience, not control the outcome.

God doesn't need perfection. He works through flawed people in imperfect circumstances. And just like with Rebekah, your transformation and purpose are secure in His hands, regardless of your imperfection.

The Cost of The Promise

Rebekah's story of transformation and truth is both powerful and sobering. The dream Rebekah received did come to pass. Just as God revealed to her, Isaac ended up blessing Jacob instead of Esau. However, the fulfilment of this divine promise came through an act of manipulation and deception—one that carried a heavy cost.

Sometimes, the very thing God calls us to will demand more from us than we anticipate. The path to purpose may come wrapped in pain. For Rebekah, her actions led to deep family conflict. It caused Esau and Jacob to be at odds for years, fuelled by betrayal and bitterness. Rebekah, who loved her son deeply, was separated from Jacob, never to see him again. And Jacob, though blessed, entered a season of hardship, serving under his uncle Laban, who deceived him just as he had once deceived his father.

"The journey to the promise
can come with great personal cost."

The promise was fulfilled—but not without a price. It's crucial to recognize that walking in God's will does not always mean walking a smooth or painless road. God is sovereign, and His plans will come to pass, even through flawed methods, even amid our mistakes. But we must not be naïve: the journey to the promise can come with great personal cost. Still, the lesson remains: don't let go of God's promises. Press forward, even when the process is uncomfortable, unclear, or unorthodox. In Christ, you are His child, His creation, made for a purpose. And while it is natural to long for the glory of the promise, you must also be prepared to walk through the story that leads to it.

Yes, transformation is beautiful, but it is also messy. The path to purpose rarely looks like what we expect. Rebekah was no longer just a mother; she became the matriarch of a nation. Jacob was no longer just the younger son; he became the father of the twelve tribes of Israel.

"Know that all things are working together
for the good of those who love the Lord and
are called according to His purpose"

ROMANS 8 VS 28

This story reminds us that transformation is not always comfortable, but it is always meaningful. You may have to grow through difficulty, evolve through struggle, and be refined by fire—but trust this: God is at work in every part of your journey.

Whatever He has spoken over your life, it will come to pass. Even if the path is unconventional, God will still accomplish His will. And when your life is transformed, it won't just impact you—it will shift your entire family, your legacy, and the generations that follow.

So, hold on. Trust the process. Know that all things are working together for the good of those who love the Lord and are called according to His purpose (Romans 8:28). On a personal level, I understand that God does not work on my time, nor does He do things the way I expect. It is clear to me that He is God with all power—He is all-knowing and ever-sovereign.

"God is the author of my destiny, and His way is best."

Hence, I endeavour to submit to His will. I had pre-planned whom to marry, what age to marry, my career—everything. Yet here I am, living the life God wanted. Who would have thought I would wait ten years to have children? Who would have thought I would be preaching? Who would have known I would be a writer?

God is the author of my destiny, and His way is best. I have surrendered to becoming who He wants me to be!

Becoming Her Check- In

Reflect:

Rebekah's journey reminds us that God's promises are true—even when the path is unfamiliar, uncomfortable, or unconventional. She teaches us the power of discernment, courage, and listening to the voice of God for ourselves. Take a moment to reflect on the posture of your heart in seasons of waiting and uncertainty.

- *Are you positioning yourself to hear clearly from God, even when His plans challenge your understanding?*
- *Have you tried to "help" God fulfil His promise in your own way instead of trusting His timing?*
- *Are you willing to release control and allow God's purpose to unfold—even when it looks different from what you expected?*

God may be calling you to trust His word, even if it means going against tradition, expectation, or your own timeline. Just like Rebekah, your decisions carry weight. They can shape not only your future, but also the legacy you leave behind.

Pray:

"Lord, give me the strength to listen, the wisdom to wait, and the courage to obey—even when the path is unorthodox. I trust that Your will is greater than my plan."

Time of Meditation

No one is perfect, but we should all strive to live a life that is pleasing to God. Rebekah is the epitome of imperfection— yet she remained within the will of God. We need to understand that God's will is sovereign. Through His word, we learn to trust God and lean not on our own understanding.

Scriptures

❖

Jeremiah 29:11
"For I know the thoughts that I think toward you, saith the Lord, thoughts of peace, and not of evil, to give you an expected end"

Romans 8:28
"And we know that all things work together for good to them that love God, to them who are the called according to his purpose."

Ephesians 1:11
"In whom also we have obtained an inheritance, being predestinated according to the purpose of him who worketh all things after the counsel of his own will"

Romans 13: 1
Let every soul be subject unto the higher powers. For there is no power but of God: the powers that be are ordained of God.

Action Steps to
Transformation

Are you listening for God's voice in the chaos—and do you trust what He's spoken over your life, even if others don't understand it?

God gave Rebekah insight into the future of her children and the promise they carried. Transformation requires confidence in what God has revealed to you, even when others can't yet see it.

_____

_____

_____

_____

_____

_____

_____

_____

_____

_____

_____

_____

_____

_____

Action Steps to
Transformation

What acts of quiet obedience and service are you being called to that could unlock your next level of purpose?

Rebekah's destiny was revealed through a simple act of kindness at a well.

Don't underestimate the power of humility and service; your breakthrough may be hidden in what seems small or unseen.

_____

_____

_____

_____

_____

_____

_____

_____

_____

_____

_____

_____

Action Steps to
Transformation

Are you willing to say "yes" to God's calling, even when the path is unfamiliar or uncomfortable?
Rebekah left everything familiar—her home, her family, her culture—to walk into the unknown by faith. Transformation often begins with surrender. Are you ready to trust God beyond your comfort zone?

_____

_____

_____

_____

_____

_____

_____

_____

_____

_____

_____

_____

_____

A
PRAYER
For You!

Heavenly Father,
We come before Your presence today, and I lift up my sister
as she embarks on this sacred journey of transformation. Let
the story of Rebekah—the woman, the wife, the mother, the
matriarch—resonate deeply in her heart. May Rebekah's
strength, faith, obedience, and boldness be a reflection of
what You are cultivating in her.

Just as Rebekah heard Your voice in the midst of
uncertainty, I pray my sister will pause, enter Your presence,
and truly listen. Speak to her, Lord. Give her clarity and
direction for her life and purpose. Remind her that she is
being transformed—not just for herself, but for others. You
are shaping her to impact generations. Strengthen her faith
and speak a word into her spirit that will anchor her through
the process.

Let her walk boldly in truth, confident in who she is
becoming. As she surrenders to Your will, help her embrace
every part of what You've fortified her with. May she be
bold like Rebekah—trusting that if You've called her,
You've also prepared her.

Bless her, Lord. Reassure her of Your plans. Remind her
that she is chosen, called, and deeply loved.

In Jesus' name, Amen.

Clarity

Key Takeaways

Transformation

✓ God is Sovereign, and he can accomplish what he sets out to do

✓ Even with our imperfections, he can fulfill promises

✓ Transformation may not be easy, but it is worth it

Becoming Her: Bold

Rebekah, bold in belief and swift in spirit, stepped into the unknown with unwavering trust, becoming her through unorthodox transformation, divinely led and destined.

notes

Leah

Transformed in the Midst of Rejection

Leah lived her life consistently facing rejection, and in the midst of that rejection, she decided it was time to shift and be transformed.

The Pain of Rejection

This is a story that we all can relate to from the vantage point that no one likes rejection. Leah's life story was knitted with different narratives—love, marriage, sibling rivalry—all intertwined with rejection. Leah lived a life that was filled with rejection, which, without a doubt, caused her to carry a great deal of emotional pain and disappointment. Whether obvious to those around her or not, her heart constantly filtered the rejected moments she experienced daily. You and I can only imagine how that affected her esteem, creating a void with a deep sense of unworthiness, undermining who she was and how undervalued she felt as a woman, leaving her desperately seeking love, validation, affection, and acceptance—especially from those closest to her, most of all her husband, Jacob.

114

Leah was married to Jacob, but the backdrop of their marriage was laced with deception. Her father had tricked Jacob into marrying his older daughter instead of the younger and more beautiful Rachel, whom Jacob loved deeply. After an agreement between Laban and Jacob, who had worked seven years to marry Rachel, the true love of his life, Laban cunningly switched Rachel for Leah on the wedding night. The switch was only discovered by Jacob the next morning. Leah's first rejection was suffered at the hands of her father, who felt the need to deceive a man in order to marry her off. This echoed what was already in her heart: that she was not wanted, that she was not desirable, especially in comparison to her younger sister.

"When my father and my mother forsake me, then the LORD will take me up."

PSLAM 27 VS 10

It is important that as we go through life and face various circumstances—even rejection—we remain mindful not to carry them as our own. We need to categorize what belongs to us and what belongs to others. How you choose to respond to any situation belongs to you. On the other hand, what others say, think, or do belongs to them.

We must not base our value system on the opinions, thoughts, or behaviours of others. It does not matter who carries these opinions—mother, father, siblings, spouses, or even our leaders. It is God's opinion that carries the defining factor of who you are and who you will become. God has never forsaken you, nor will He ever, even amid His silence.

115

The Rivalry

Unlike most people, I have never experienced sibling rivalry firsthand, but currently, I live it vicariously through my children. The rivalry between these two sisters was epic and painful. The pain of Leah's rejection riddled all her relationships, fostering an unhealthy rivalry with her sister.

Now that Leah was married—and her husband saw it fit to work another seven years to marry her younger sister —this act was a resounding statement that reminded Leah: You are not the one I truly love. Jacob's love for Rachel caused him to work those seven years with ease, as if they were just a few days to him. This act amplified his love for Rachel and the time he was willing to invest away from Leah. Again, Leah's heart was at the mercy of her husband.

"Leah was tender eyed; but Rachel was beautiful and well favoured."

GENESIS 29 VS 17

Though it was customary to have several wives, to know that it was your sister who had the affection of your husband was unimaginable and heartbreaking. Not only was Leah compared to Rachel and quantified as less beautiful—she was also less favoured and least preferred.

Rejected but not forgotten

Sometimes in our thoughts or perception, we internalize our pain and rejection. As a result, we tend to project and count ourselves out, labelling ourselves as not worthy and not valuable. But God is the one who places value on who we are, not ourselves, not our pain, and not those around us. We are a royal priesthood, a holy nation. We are created in the image of God and in His likeness. Therefore, we should allow God to transform our thinking and order our steps so we can come into full recognition of who we are, and not what our pain dictates. We should never buy into the narrative of what our pain or trauma causes us to feel.

> *"Leah was divinely chosen by God, despite her deep-seated rejection."*

Regardless of Leah's pain and how downtrodden she felt, God saw it fit to bless Leah with children while her more beautiful, loved sister was barren. Though this is not a moment to celebrate Rachel's misfortune of barrenness, it is a moment to highlight the favour on Leah's life. Leah was divinely chosen by God, despite her deep-seated rejection. Know that you are chosen by God Himself, and when your mind is renewed, you will be able to walk in your divine purpose and the perfect will of God! Once Leah's mind was transformed, her thinking and her attitude followed.

117

After having several children—sons, to be precise—and still not able to win the full affection of her husband, still playing second fiddle to her younger sister, Leah has a transformative moment. She decides that she will no longer focus on man's love but instead focus on God's love. Judah was her fourth son. She named him Judah, as she decided, "I will place my praise and my affection on the One who loves!"

When we allow God to influence our thinking, we are also allowing Him to override every negative emotion that we may carry, allowing Him to soothe our hearts and heal us.

Through her pain, she learned to praise God until she was transformed into a new woman. No longer prioritizing the need to be loved by her husband, she shifted her full affection to the One who had loved her from the very beginning. Her energy was no longer misplaced—God now had her full attention. He was the One who blessed her womb and understood her worth as both a mother and a woman. In response, she praised Him and monumentalized that praise by naming her son Judah.

Like many other women, including a few in your circle, when we have an encounter with God, we are allowing ourselves to experience the miraculous blessing of the Lord operating in our lives. Leah began to put her focus on the One who mattered—the God of her salvation. As a result, she gave birth to six of the founding fathers of the tribes of Israel. God saw the pain and the rejection that Leah faced and chose to open her womb while her rival and sister remained barren despite their human efforts.

It was Leah's perseverance, despite her desperation for affection, that pushed her through to being engrafted into the legacy of something bigger than her pain—bigger than her rejection.

Rejected but Transformed

Leah's transformation was epic, but also something she took control over after suffering for so many years, looking for love and acceptance from people who could not give it to her.
It was when she looked to God and stopped focusing on others—when she began to shower God with love, adoration, and praises—that she was finally able to see herself as God saw her. When Leah began to walk in her transformed self and put her faith in God, she was able to see her blessing.

She had most of Jacob's sons, regardless of her unfavourable position as a wife. Jacob's final resting place was next to Leah, despite not being loved by him. She mothered Levi, who was the head of the priestly tribe, one of the most prominent tribes of Israel. In addition, she was the mother of Judah, who was not only of the kingly lineage but also the lineage of Jesus, our Saviour. As epic as her pain and rejection were, her transformation gave way to her realizing she was raising kings and priestly men and holding prominence in biblical history.

As a young lady, I grew up with that feeling of rejection and abandonment, which amplified my emotional trauma in my youthful days. At eleven years old, I met Jesus Christ. I remember crying out so desperately for Him to save me. Though I did not have the words or the wit to put all the puzzle pieces together, something inside of me knew I needed Christ to step in—and that He did. It was at that moment that my transformation process began. I was never the same. It took many years of realization.

119

I have endeavoured to praise God like Leah, not out of my pain, but despite my pain, hurt, and disappointments—because He deserves it all. It was on my journey of becoming her, the new version of myself.

Leah not only carried her praise in her womb, she gave birth to her praise and declared, "Now I will praise the Lord. "Let us now become like Leah and carry, birth, and declare our praise, Hallelujah!

Becoming Her Check-In

Reflect:

1. *What labels have you accepted that God never gave you?*
2. *Leah believed she wasn't enough, but God saw her. Write down the false labels you carry and replace them with God's truth.*
3. *Where have you sought love or validation that only God can give?*
4. *Have you been striving for acceptance from others? Invite God to fill that space.*
5. *Can you praise in your pain?*
6. *Leah's breakthrough came when she chose to praise. What does it look like for you to praise God in this season?*

Remember:

Rejection may wound, but it cannot redefine you. When you place your worth in God's hands, even the most painful places can birth legacy. Let praise rise from the place of pain—there, transformation begins.

Time of Meditation

It is time we take a moment and meditate on the scriptures—on how much God loves us—and come to the understanding that it is through accepting His unconditional love that we can begin the process of transformation.

Meditate on the scriptures and know this: God's plan for your life is not limited by what others think, say, or how they behave toward you. It is only limited by how big you see God!

Scriptures

---◆---

Psalms 27:10
"When my father and my mother forsake me, then the LORD will take me up."

Genesis 29:31
"And when the LORD saw that Leah was hated, he opened her womb: but Rachel was barren."

Genesis 29:35
"And she conceived again, and bare a son: and she said, Now will I praise the LORD: therefore she called his name Judah; and left bearing."

Romans 8:37-39
"Nay, in all these things we are more than conquerors through him that loved us. For I am persuaded, that neither death, nor life, nor angels, nor principalities, nor powers, nor things present, nor things to come, Nor height, nor depth, nor any other creature, shall be able to separate us from the love of God, which is in Christ Jesus our Lord."

Action Steps to
Transformation

Have you ever felt rejected and unloved? How did you handle it and how were you able to move forward positively?

_____

_____

_____

_____

_____

_____

_____

_____

_____

_____

_____

_____

_____

_____

_____

_____

Action Steps to
Transformation

Like Leah, you may have felt abandoned or rejected by a loved one and found yourself constantly looking for their affection and validation.

I invite you to take a moment for honest introspection and reflect on the ways God has already favoured you. Begin to list some of the beautiful and undeniable ways He has demonstrated His love for you.

_____

_____

_____

_____

_____

_____

_____

_____

_____

_____

_____

_____

_____

_____

_____

Action Steps to
Transformation

Like Leah, you may have felt abandoned or rejected by a loved one and found yourself constantly looking for their affection and validation.

I invite you to take a moment for honest introspection and reflect on the ways God has already favoured you. Begin to list some of the beautiful and undeniable ways He has demonstrated His love for you.

_____

_____

_____

_____

_____

_____

_____

_____

_____

_____

_____

_____

Action Steps to
Transformation

Because we believe that we are transformed to transform, I encourage you to pour into someone's life by uplifting them with words of affirmation.

Sometimes, when we give to others that which we are expecting, we open a door of divine reciprocity.

A
PRAYER
For You!

Dear Lord,
I thank You for my dear sister today. I join my faith with hers as we come before You, seeking not only forgiveness but restoration.
Lord, we ask for forgiveness for allowing the thoughts of others to shape our opinion of ourselves rather than looking to You.
We now ask that You restore our minds and renew our thinking so we can begin to put our focus on You—the One who matters most.
We invite the Holy Spirit to comfort our hearts that have experienced the trauma of rejection and abandonment.
May the Holy Spirit help us process these emotions, shift our perspective, and forgive those who have contributed to these feelings.
Lord, we pray that as we lean on Your Word and Your love for us, we will walk through the process of transformation and live as valued, loved, purpose-filled women of God.
In Jesus' name, Amen.

Restoration

Key Takeaways

Transformation

✓ Your Purpose is in Christ, not in man

✓ God's value in you always overrides what others place on you.

✓ Your transformation may come through your moments of rejection

---

Becoming Her: Worthy

She praised through the pain and rose from rejection—because even when overlooked by man, she was always worthy to God.

notes

Ruth

Transformed Through Mentorship

Ruth was a Moabite who came to live in Bethlehem with her mother-in-law. Through her willingness to be mentored, she brought transformation to both their lives.

Loving through Tragedy

Ruth, a Moabite woman, met and married the son of Naomi. After loving and losing her husband unexpectedly, Ruth did not allow her tragedy to limit her from moving forward. She embarked on a journey of humility and determination.

We must understand that, as a Moabite, she was culturally different. They served other gods and practiced different faiths. After the tragedy of losing her husband, Naomi decided to return to Bethlehem and encouraged Ruth to go back to her family. This is where we get a glimpse of Ruth aligning herself with Naomi, a Jewish woman—evidence that Ruth was already on a journey of transformation.

Ruth forcefully rejected Naomi's encouragement to return home during their time of mourning.

''And Ruth said, Intreat me not to leave thee, or to return from following after thee: for whither thou goest, I will go; and where thou lodgest, I will lodge: thy people shall be my people, and thy God my God:''

RUTH 1 VS 16

———————————

She announced that she would not leave but would instead remain with Naomi, choosing to bond through their shared tragedy and love for each other. Ruth declared her dedication to live and die with Naomi, to serve Naomi's God, and to be counted among her people.

Ruth could have chosen what might have seemed like an easier path by returning to her home. Instead, she chose to be a stranger in a foreign land, among people who would most likely not welcome her. Though tragedy brought these two women together, their love and loyalty created an unbreakable bond. Ruth's choice revealed the heart of a polytheistic woman being transformed to serve the one true God—Jehovah—most likely introduced to her through marriage and her mother-in-law's example.

Her newfound faith and commitment were not only to Naomi but also to God. Ruth was a woman of deep loyalty and unwavering bravery, willing to journey into the unknown. As transformed women, we must fully embrace our faith and demonstrate a heart that is resolute in its commitment to God. Our lives should be a visible example to those who encounter us.

Ruth the Outsider

Ruth arrived in Bethlehem with her mother-in-law, not knowing what would happen next, but she stood steadfast, holding on to their love and the hope they had in God. It would take extraordinary character to embrace her new home and new people. Ruth would need to look beyond her limitations and act with bravery to do what it took to survive and assist her mother-in-law. Ruth's circumstances now required her to make decisions and live a transformational life daily. Ruth was intentionally choosing a path of transformation. She worked hard, went out daily, and gleaned—as was customary for an outsider—unbothered by what others might think of her. She was driven by love and loyalty. Ruth found favour and was able to gain extra for their upkeep.

"So she kept fast by the maidens of Boaz to glean unto the end of barley harvest and of wheat harvest; and dwelt with her mother in law."

RUTH 2 VS 23

As a result of her intentionality and care for her mother-in-law, Ruth's reputation grew in Bethlehem. People in the community noticed her godly characteristics, which echoed throughout her reputation—a woman loyal, hardworking, caring, loving, and faithful. She was being transformed from an outsider filled with heartbreak into a reputable young woman in her newfound community.

131

She found favour with Boaz, favour with the workmen in the fields, and was apparently looked upon favourably by the other women. She was now transforming into a valued member of the community of Bethlehem.

Transformed through mentorship.

The relationship between Ruth and Naomi was beyond that of a mother and daughter; it was a relationship of mentor to mentee. After their loss and tragedy, they found a deep level of connection during a time when they needed each other most. With no husbands or children, they had to lean on each other to get through their difficulties. Now that Ruth was in an environment unfamiliar to her—both culturally and religiously—she needed someone to guide her in navigating this new way of life. It was likely Naomi who guided her to glean in the fields so they could eat.

Once Naomi learned that Ruth had found favour in Boaz's field, she encouraged Ruth to continue, informing her that Boaz was a relative-a family redeemer, according to custom. As a redeemer, Boaz would have the right to buy back their property and marry the widow in order to carry on the family lineage and protect the inheritance.

"And she said unto her, All that thou sayest unto me I will do."

RUTH 3 VS 5

Naomi, knowing that there would be a time when she would no longer be around to take care of Ruth, saw it fit to guide her in securing her future. We see this plan unfold in the scriptures, where Naomi strategically instructed Ruth on exactly what to do—meeting with Boaz and proposing marriage to him, as dictated by their culture. This plan may seem unconventional to us, but it was customary in their time.

This was an act of bravery and faith. Ruth followed through with her mother-in-law's directions and was able to gain the affection and commitment of Boaz. In other words, the plan worked. It was Ruth's boldness, combined with Naomi's mentorship, that caused them both to be redeemed by Boaz.

We should not underestimate the need to mentor the young ladies under our care. It was through mentorship that Ruth was fully transformed into a woman who was trustworthy in a culture and society unfamiliar to her. She gained the respect of the community and the favour of Boaz, even as a foreigner.

It became evident to everyone that she was able to adapt completely to their culture and customs, which ultimately secured Naomi and Ruth's future. Ruth gave birth to Obed, the grandfather of King David, a direct link to the lineage of Jesus Christ, our Lord and Saviour.

"Her willingness to be mentored by Naomi was key to her transformation."

Each of us—our transformation will look and come to us in different ways. Nonetheless, we must seize every opportunity to share our faith and testimonies with those we encounter. We are transformed to help others gain truth and knowledge so they can better navigate through their transformation. Imagine Naomi not sharing her customs and knowledge, not being transparent with Ruth. Both of them would have continued to live in a state of poverty, depending on the kindness of others. Instead, they were redeemed, and all that was rightfully theirs was restored to them. Ruth, a Moabite by origin, is now linked to all the matriarchs of Israel and the foremother of our Messiah.

Through my process of transformation, I have not only seized the opportunity to mentor others but have also shared with them the opportunity to serve alongside me. I cannot allow disappointment and tragedy to stop me from moving forward and becoming who God wants me to be. It was through a moment of disappointment that our hospitality ministry was born. It was out of difficulties in my marriage that God created a compassion for other wives, which allowed Him to trust me with starting our Wives Connect group. Through these moments in life, I choose to allow them to transform me so I can support others.

Ruth was transformed from a Moabite woman into the ancestry of King Jesus—transformed from a polytheistic religion to serving and living a life of faith in Jehovah, the God of Israel. Alongside Ruth, Naomi was transformed from bitterness to a woman filled with hope, able to take her grandchild into her arms.

They both experienced loss and tragedy and are now living transformed lives of redemption. Ruth's willingness to be mentored by Naomi was key to her transformation. I encourage you to know your Naomi and honour their role in your life.

Becoming Her Check- In

> *Reflect:*
> **Have you fully embraced your transformation like Ruth—stepping forward in faith, loyalty, and purpose, even when the future feels uncertain?**
> **Your becoming may begin in loss, but it unfolds through love, trust, and courageous obedience.**
>
>
> *Remember:*
> *Transformation sometimes begins in the soil of sorrow. Like Ruth, your path may start in unfamiliar territory, but when you walk in loyalty, humility, and faith, God will order your steps. Don't underestimate the quiet strength of obedience or the divine favour that follows a willing heart. Stay faithful in the gleaning— redemption is often found in the fields of daily sacrifice.*

Time of Meditation

During this time of meditation, take the time to reflect on God's word and the story of Ruth—a woman of great dedication, loyalty, and unwavering love. Look past all your tragedies and create a path to move forward, knowing that God's love for you is also sacrificial.

Scriptures

---❖---

Titus 2:3
The aged women likewise, that they be in behaviour as becometh holiness, not false accusers, not given to much wine, teachers of good things;

Proverbs 17:17
A friend loveth at all times, and a brother is born for adversity.

Ruth 1:16
And Ruth said, Intreat me not to leave thee, or to return from following after thee: for whither thou goest, I will go; and where thou lodgest, I will lodge: thy people shall be my people, and thy God my God.

John 3:16
For God so loved the world, that he gave his only begotten Son, that whosoever believeth in him should not perish, but have everlasting life

Action Steps to
Transformation

We all have faced some sort of tragedy in our lives. In spite of these tragedies, as transformed women, we must endeavour to move forward and not allow them to hinder our growth in becoming God's leading ladies. Identify any tragedy—small or great—and begin to formulate a plan on how to move forward.

Action Steps to
Transformation

Ruth had Naomi. Who is your Naomi? Naomi represents that older female in your life whom you are able to align yourself with and give permission to speak into your life—someone whose instruction you can trust during your journey of transformation. Feel free to list these ladies below as you identify them. And yes, I said ladies, as you may be blessed to identify more than one.

_____

_____

_____

_____

_____

_____

_____

_____

_____

_____

_____

_____

Action Steps to
Transformation

One aspect of this story I loved is the loyalty that Ruth had toward Naomi. She embraced who Naomi was and who Naomi was becoming. She did not let the tragedy shift her out of becoming her. Rather, she dug her heels in and made a declaration of a covenant relationship. Oh yes, are you able to identify your Ruth? The ladies who will not leave you in the midst of your tragedy. List their names below, endeavour to pray for them, and communicate to them how much you value them in your life.

_____

_____

_____

_____

_____

_____

_____

_____

_____

_____

A
PRAYER
For You!

Lord, I come to You, giving You thanks in all
things and for all things.
We thank You for saving us. You are our God,
and today I beseech You as our Redeemer.
I pray that You will redeem my sister from her
past into her destiny as she journeys through the
process of transformation. Help my sister to
recognize that You are the only one who holds
the key to providentially unlock her destiny.
You are able to bring the right persons into her
path—those who will mentor and guide her into
alignment with Your will. Send someone who
will support her, cover her in prayer, and nurture
her divine characteristics—someone of reputable
integrity.
Highlight everything that is good about her, that
it may attract her destiny helpers—in her career,
in her relationships, and in her spiritual walk
with You.
Lord, I commit and submit my sister into Your
hands.
Amen.

Redeemed

Key Takeaways

Transformation

✓ Willing to be mentored

✓ Dedicated and Loyalty

✓ Hard working and commitment

Becoming Her: Aligned

She didn't wait for permission—she walked in divine authority, and the nation followed.

notes

Deborah

A Transformed Leader

~~~~~~

Deborah was a wife, prophetess, and judge during the time of the judges. She was unique—the first and only female leader of Israel, as well as the judge of Israel. One of the very few people who carried the responsibility of both prophet and judge, her authority at that time came directly from God. She was hand-picked, not voted in. Positions were not inherited; they were divinely appointed. Deborah was called and chosen by God Himself in a society predominantly led by men. What a powerhouse!

Divine Influence

Deborah is now one of my favourite women in the Bible. The more I listened to stories and read about her, the more I fell in love with who she was as a woman and as a leader. Deborah showed up in the Bible already transformed; we did not get to witness her transformation or read of it. Nonetheless, we can read the chronicle of how she lived her life as a transformed leader through the scriptures. In addition, we can see how she helped the Israelites through a period of transformation.

Deborah was unique in that she was a leader during a time when women leading and giving instructions to men was extremely unpopular.

Her role embodied a prophetess who gave the message of God, both foretelling and forthtelling. She was a judge who helped the people resolve their issues both spiritually and personally. As a judge, she led the Israelites because they did not have a king at that time. She was a wife, and outside of these roles, she is not known to be from a family of affluence, but she was chosen by God.

Being chosen by God is all that she needed—and it should be all that you and I need.

"She was respected and sought after because of her gift and her influence."

As a transformed leader, Deborah exhibited various characteristics that are reputable and should be modelled. Deborah had influence. When you are living a transformed life, you will have influence. Though it was part of her responsibility to judge the Israelites, the people came to her daily and sought her help. She did not go looking for what to do or whom to assist—they came to her.

Her influence caused the people to come seeking her assistance. She was respected and sought after due to her gift and influence. In our current day and time, influencers are popular and widely followed on social media platforms. If we're honest, many of these influencers go through various means to gain followers. Deborah's reputation and skill made room for her. She was sought after and recognized as an influential leader.

As transformed women and leaders in our context, we need to possess reputable characteristics that allow us to influence others in the will of God. People must seek us out for godly counsel.

They should be drawn to us because there is something within us that will help them grow, improve, and walk into their purpose. We cannot be influencers simply for popularity's sake—there must be a God-given purpose within us that others can access.

We must be ready, so others can tap into what God has placed in us to help them become the transformed individuals they are called to be.

"When you are transformed, you can lift others and push them into their destiny'

Deborah experienced success in her life, and the people around her were aware of it. They recognized that what she had to offer was both good and divinely inspired. She was competent and qualified in her God-given ability to offer guidance that would lead others to success and spiritual fulfilment.

It wasn't just the general population who sought her out—other leaders did too. Although she was not a soldier, Deborah was invited to join the military in battle. Barak, the military commander at the time, specifically requested her presence when it was time to go into battle. If Deborah had a poor reputation or lacked meaningful influence, the people would not have come to her daily, nor would other leaders have sought her support in fulfilling their responsibilities.

When you are transformed, you are empowered to uplift others and propel them into their own destinies.

A Character of Consistency

Can we talk about her impeccable characteristics? Deborah demonstrated consistency. She earned the respect of her community through her steadfast commitment to her role. When the people needed her, they knew exactly where to find her. She had a set place to meet them and carry out her duties as a judge—she sat beneath the palm tree that came to bear her name. Her unwavering presence and faithful service under that same tree, day after day, was so notable that it became a landmark of her consistency.

As transformed women of God and leaders, we must embrace consistency in fulfilling our God-given missions. We are called by God, and it is through obedience and consistency that we carry out His divine will for our lives. This faithfulness not only allows us to walk in our purpose but creates space for others to walk in theirs. We cannot afford to show up one day and be missing the next. Consistency is key to being a transformed leader.

We cannot hide our gifts or skills and expect to make a divine impact. Deborah did not hide behind her role as a wife or mother—she cared for her household while showing up for her community. She unwaveringly answered the call of God on her life and walked in obedience daily. Others are depending on us. We are each called to someone and for something.

Let us not allow inconsistency or disobedience to cause us to miss the mark of God. Through consistency, we build trust with those we are called to lead. As transformed leaders, we must endeavour to create a legacy of faithfulness so that others can trust our leadership and follow us into divine truth.

146

Deborah's leadership and influence had a powerful impact, helping her people move from defeat to victory, from spiritual brokenness to restoration.

The Warrior

"Where no counsel is, the people fall: but in the multitude of counsellors there is safety."

PROVERBS 11 VS 14

The Israelites went through an overwhelming time of oppression, as God had given neighbouring kingdoms rule over them due to their repeated disobedience and idolatry. During Deborah's era, they faced oppression for twenty years. They began to cry out to God for deliverance, and it was during that time we see where she sent for the leader of the army, Barak.

As a prophetess, she called Barak and foretold him what God had already spoken to him regarding going forth and fighting the battle. She proceeded to foretell him of the victory of the battle. Deborah's gift as a prophetess was in high motion, but we can see her gift of wisdom in action as well. It was through her wisdom that she approached Barak, the seasoned veteran who was responsible for leading the army.

It was wisdom in operation when she told him what he already knew—what God had instructed. She did not call him to rebuke him or deal with him harshly. She was wise in putting God's word first and not her opinion, by letting him know what God said.

147

She was not condemning but uplifting and reassuring, by foretelling the pending victory they would obtain once they went to war.

Israel experienced transformation and deliverance through the victory of this war, breaking free from 20 years of oppression. It was under the incredible leadership of Deborah that this victory was possible. The people prayed, and God answered by sending them a female leader who trusted Him and wisely guided them to victory.

It may not be necessary, but can we put some emphasis on the fact that she was a female leader? Many may judge us women and exclude us from many arenas and hold the door closed to our gifts, but not God; He is all-inclusive.

Standing by Her Prophecy

It is safe to say that Deborah, the wife, Deborah the prophetess, Deborah the judge, did not need to go to war, but she chose to. As leaders, we need to know when to stand with our people. We need to walk the talk and walk in confidence in what God has spoken. Deborah stood by what God prophesied to her. Barak trusted her, and he presented her with an opportunity to show up for the people—with the people—standing in the confidence of what she knew to be true. It was as if Deborah was saying, "God said it, and I know He will do it!"

Do you have the confidence to stand on the Word of God in unfavourable circumstances? She had nothing to lose, nothing to fear. As transformed leaders, we need to show up and demonstrate to the people what it looks like to stand on the Word of God amid difficult times, amid battles, amid oppression. 148

The enemy might have had the upper hand for years, they might have the larger army, they might have the better equipment—but we have a resounding word of VICTORY from God. God's Word will be our weapon; it will be our marching order. His Word will be our courage that takes us into battle—and into victory.

Transformed leaders lead by example and show up with the people.

Transformation and Deliverance

We can resolve that she was a remarkably wise leader of her time who broke the norms of her society. It was her remarkable attributes that brought the children of Israel through a transformative time—from being oppressed to being delivered. She did not just impact the people individually; she was able to bring transformation to an entire nation that suffered under the oppressive rule of neighbouring kingdoms. She led with God's wisdom, using only the Word of God as her guide and means of instruction. Her faith and trust in God were evident as she accompanied the army to war, all the while demonstrating her support and leadership.

We did not see Deborah's transformation, but we are able to witness the transformation of those around her. Jael becomes a hero. Barak, the captain of the army, won the war. The Israelites cried out to God in repentance. Deborah followed God's will with precision. Transformation not only affects you—it also affects those around you.

It is my desire to carry out the will of God for my life and the mandate He entrusted me with, with precision. The Transformation Conference is such a great example of me carrying out the mandate according to the precise vision God placed in my heart and mind.

My desire is what God wants: to see the lives of women in Montreal elevated, for women to rise up and be who God called them to be, to break the limitations of our mindset and walk in the fullness of our giftings and calling. No more limits!

Be ye TRANSFORMED!

Becoming Her Check-In

Reflect:

Are you boldly walking in the authority God has given you? Deborah didn't wait for permission—she moved with clarity, consistency, and confidence. Are you rooted in your identity enough to lead with wisdom, to speak what God says, and to show up even when the battle looks bigger than you?

Remember:

Your authority doesn't come from the approval of people—it comes from the assignment of God. Like Deborah, stand firm in who He called you to be. Your wisdom, your voice, and your leadership are needed right where you are.

Time of Meditation

Let us meditate on who we are called to be, and how God can guide us—through the power of the Holy Spirit—to become exactly that. One significant truth we must understand is that we have a role to play in becoming who God has called us to be. We also have a role to play in accomplishing our mission. How do we do that? By asking, seeking, and responding with obedience. Read the following scriptures and meditate on them as you ask, seek, and find.

Scriptures

Matthew 6: 33
But seek ye first the kingdom of God, and his righteousness; and all these things shall be added unto you

Luke 11:9
And I say unto you, Ask, and it shall be given you; seek, and ye shall find; knock, and it shall be opened unto you.

Proverbs 11:14
Where no counsel is, the people fall: but in the multitude of counsellors there is safety.

Psalm 78: 72
So he fed them according to the integrity of his heart, and guided them by the skillfulness of his hands.

Action Steps to
Transformation

As a transformed leader, we see Deborah demonstrate a prominent level of consistency by showing up daily and serving the people of Israel. What are some ways you can improve—or are you already showing up daily as a leader?

_____
_____
_____
_____
_____
_____
_____
_____
_____
_____
_____
_____
_____
_____

Action Steps to
Transformation

As we have seen, who we are is deeply connected to how we show up in society. What are some of the characteristics you can identify in Deborah's life that you also see reflected in your own? How do those traits show up in your daily life?

_____

_____

_____

_____

_____

_____

_____

_____

_____

_____

_____

_____

_____

Action Steps to
Transformation

Deborah brought transformation to the lives of those around her. In what ways are you impacting the lives of the people God has called you to? Are you answering the call like Deborah—walking in obedience—or are you more like Barak, who heard God but needed confirmation?

Take time to reflect. Work through your thoughts and write a commitment letter to God, outlining how you desire to move forward in responding to your mission or missions, especially in helping others experience their transformation, just as Deborah did.

_____

_____

_____

_____

_____

_____

_____

_____

_____

_____

A
PRAYER
For You!

Our Lord and our Saviour,
I ask in the mighty name of Jesus for my
sister as she walks through her
transformation. I pray that she will
continuously give You room in her life to
demonstrate Your power. May she always
make space for You to sharpen her gift.
I pray that as she engages in her calling
daily, You will establish her and cause her
gift to make room for her in all her ways.
Show her how to trust You, trust Your
Word, and trust Your leadership through
her.
Grace her with the anointing that will
bring both influence and consistency in her
ministry. Grace her with the oil that brings
transformation—not only in her personal
life, but in the lives of those around her.
In Jesus' name,
Amen.

Influence

Key Takeaways

Transformation

✓ Consistency is a key ingredient as a
Transformational leader

✓ Your influences should be purpose driven

✓ Be available to serve others

Becoming Her: Authority

She didn't wait for permission—she walked in divine authority, and the nation followed.

notes

You Are Her

I am moved and inspired by each of these stories of the female giants positioned in the pages of the Holy Scriptures. Their gifts are carved out by their unique personalities and the stories that brought transformation to their own lives—and to the lives of everyone reading. Their personal stories are inspiring and go far beyond the lines written in the Holy Scriptures. They are filled with flaws and successes, struggles and triumphs, lack and fear—yet overflowing with faith and obedience.

Their faith, their obedience, and their triumphs move me to want to grow, evolve, and transform into someone new, with the hope of inspiring you, too.

When you allow God to use you and invite His transforming power to work in your life, you can effect change not just for yourself but for others. You can become the woman who shifts atmospheres, speaks life, nurtures nations, saves lives like Zipporah, and gives birth to future world changers.

We must be intentional about our actions and walk in obedience. The gifts that God has given us are not just for ourselves—they are to be used to elevate others in our communities and within our circles of influence. We must always be ready and willing. Our character should reflect that of a godly woman being renewed and transformed. We cannot be who we were before. Our love for God is what will transform us as we strive to walk in obedience.

Just like Mary Magdalene, we must understand that God looks beyond our past—and that through His ultimate sacrifice, He has freed us from it.

A transformed life is possible. You can live a godly, fulfilled life with purpose. Your value and identity are in Christ Jesus, despite your flaws and insecurities.

It is time, as women, that we draw from each other, learn from the stories we share, and lead the way—valiantly—into a transformed life that inspires others. Let us be the modern-day Esthers, Ruths, Deborahs, Sarahs… and the list goes on.

But even more than that: You Are Her.

Becoming her doesn't mean becoming someone else—it means becoming who you were created to be in the image of God. It means drawing from the women of Scripture for the season you're in. There will be days when you need the faith of Sarah to believe the impossible. Other times, you may need to pray without ceasing, like Hannah. You may be called to lead boldly like Deborah, or serve humbly like Leah. You may be challenged to love sacrificially, like Ruth, or stand courageously, like Esther.

Whatever season you're in, understand that Becoming Her is not a destination—it's a transformational journey, only made possible through the Word of God. And when the time comes, like Esther, you will find that you have been equipped for such a time as this.

So arise, woman of God.

Be Her.

Become Her.

You already are.

Hi there

Evg. Dejah Smart-Moses, married for over two decades with two children, serves at the Resurrection Center for 20+ years. Ministering in Montreal churches, she's passionate about empowering women spiritually, guiding them to walk in their gifting and calling. Holding pastoral credentials with the COG in Christ, she oversees the ushering department and founded the Wives Connect group at Resurrection Center. With a BA in Christian Education and a Christian counseling diploma, she actively contributes to the ministry.

www.ingramcontent.com/pod-product-compliance
Lightning Source LLC
Chambersburg PA
CBHW052006090426
42741CB00008B/1568